IN SEARCH OF COLCHESTER'S PAST

by Philip Crummy

D1810550

© 1986 Colchester Archaeological Trust Ltd., 12 Lexden Road,
Colchester CO3 3NF
First edition 1979
Reprinted 1981 with minor revisions
Second edition 1984 revised and enlarged
Third edition 1986 revised and enlarged
Printed by JB Offset Printers, Marks Tey, Colchester
Artwork and camera-ready copy prepared by Colchester Archaeological Trust Ltd.
ISBN 0-9503727-5-7

PROLOGUE

Those interested in Colchester's past are fortunate in having some important historical information available to them. Although almost exclusively related to Colchester's earliest days, this information, especially that of the Roman historian, Tacitus, plays a key role in all attempts to understand Colchester's origins.

The essential details can be summarized as follows: Camulodunum (now known to be at the site of modern Colchester) was the tribal centre of the Trinovantes and was in the Roman world regarded as a principal settlement of late Iron Age Britain. Until his death in about AD 41, its chioftain was Cunobelin. During the invasion of AD 43, the Roman army headed for Camulodunum, the capture of which was its primary objective; indeed, so great was the value placed on its subjection that the emperor Claudius journeyed from Rome to lead his victorious army into the conquered settlement. To keep the peace, a fortress was established at Camulodunum and the Twentieth Legion garrisoned there. In AD 48-9 the legion was transferred to the other side of the country to fight the Silures of Wales. This was a tribe led by Caratacus, a son of Cunobelin who had escaped the Roman net in AD 43. A colony for veteran soldiers was founded in place of the legionary fortress at Camulodunum, its purposes being the promotion of the Roman way of life by example to the indigenous population and the maintenance of a strong military presence in the area. A major undertaking in the new colony was the construction of a large temple dedicated to Claudius who was worshipped as a god. In the new Roman province of Britannia, the colony at Camulodunum was unique because its inhabitants held Roman citizenship and the colony was considered to be an autonomous extension of Rome itself. The Trinovantes were naturally very resentful; their lands had been confiscated by the invaders, they were treated as slaves, and they were taxed very heavily. So when the Iceni of East Anglia, led by their queen Boudica, rose in rebellion in AD 60-1, the Trinovantes were quick to join their cause. Together they destroyed the Roman settlements at Colchester, London and St. Albans and almost shook Britain free of the hated Roman yoke. But the might and discipline of the Roman army triumphed in the end and the revolt was crushed. Although always a major town in Roman Britain, never again did Colchester figure so prominently in national terms.

THE EARLY ANTIQUARIANS

The search for Colchester's past was begun in earnest during the first part of the 18th century by the Reverend Philip Morant. His contribution was a magnificent and scholarly history of the town entitled *The History and Antiquities of Colchester*. Morant came to Colchester in 1738 to be rector of St. Mary-at-the-Walls and found in the Moot Hall (the town hall) chests full of documents which made up the Borough records. Many of these dated back to the 14th century or earlier and had previously been unexamined. These Morant pored over for some ten years and, drawing on his experience and skill as a writer and historian, he produced the first proper history of Colchester. Morant's work was inevitably biased towards the medieval and later periods since his main source was the Borough records but as far as the limited evidence would allow, he also dealt with Roman and Saxon times, including mosaic pavements and other objects of Roman date found in the town.

Morant was writing at a time when a great controversy raged over the true site of Camulodunum. Many historians followed Camden who in the 16th century had identified it with Maldon; others plumped for places such as Saffron Walden or Great Chesterford but Morant, backed up by many authorities of his time, argued forcibly that it was at Colchester. He put forward several reasons to support this theory, the most powerful of which were the frequent discoveries around the town of small coins of gold, silver, and bronze with on one side *CAM* for Camulodunum and on the other *CVN* for Cunobelin. And of course Morant was right, but unequivocal proof of this was not to emerge for almost two hundred years.

To the west of Colchester, mainly on Stanway and Lexden Heaths, are several earthworks still well enough preserved in the 18th century for one historian to describe them as 'stupendous' and to excite considerable, if sometimes eccentric, antiquarian interest. They were first surveyed in 1722 by Lufkin and Smith, whose

*Your most obedient
humble Servant

Phil Morant*

Sketch of Morant. (Courtesy of the Colchester and Essex Museum and the Essex Record Office.)

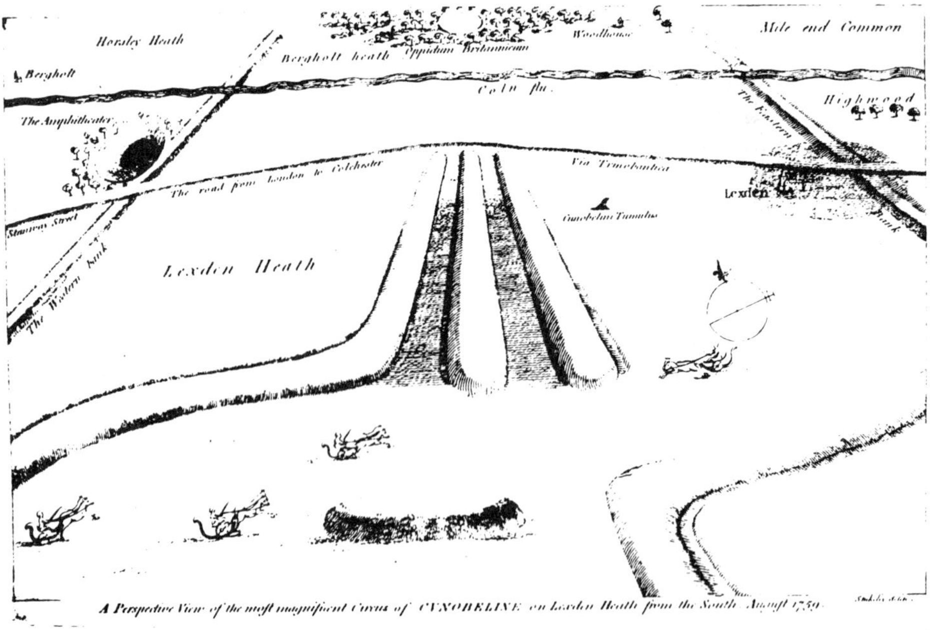

The earthworks at Lexden by William Stukeley. (Courtesy of Chelmsford Public Library.)

Iron Age coins from Colchester with CAM on one side and CVN on the other. Twice actual size.

findings formed the basis of Morant's description of them. In 1759, the earthworks attracted the attention of Dr. William Stukeley, a prominent and imaginative antiquarian, who made five drawings of them to use in his projected book on the kings of Britain, unfortunately never completed. Stukeley believed that the earthworks at Lexden included the remains of Cunobelin's circus, amphitheatre and burial place; the oval enclosure at West Bergholt (Pitchbury Ramparts) he saw as the oppidum, or settlement, of the Trinovantes. In his history a few years earlier, Morant had been more cautious and had wisely been content to describe the earthworks as simply the remains of 'camps'. As we shall see, Morant was closer to the truth than Stukeley.

Just as Morant had laid the foundations of research into Colchester's written archives, so William Wire was to do the same a hundred years later for Colchester's buried archaeological remains. Wire was a clockmaker who

4

Imaginative reconstruction of the Moot Hall c 1200, viewed from the High Street. Drawing by Peter Froste.

had served his apprenticeship in London and returned to Colchester to set up business in 1828. But his enduring passion was the archaeology of Colchester and for many years he toured the town's building sites on the lookout for archaeological material. He kept a detailed diary and some notebooks in which he recorded the discoveries of objects, buildings, and burials. From the workmen who found them, he bought many objects to add to his collection of Colchester finds. His notes and sketch plans brought a new dimension to the study of Colchester's past and set a standard of recording building works that was not to be surpassed until the 1920s.

There was much for Wire to do because at this time many works of various kinds were being undertaken in the town. Projects which feature prominently in Wire's pages are the building of the railway, quarrying for sand near Butt Road, and the laying of the first gas-mains and deep sewers.

In 1843, the town suffered a tragic loss when the Moot Hall was demolished to make way for a new town hall. During the demolition, a beautifully carved window was discovered and a rather battered carved doorway. Wire's contribution to the recording of the building was not as great as he would have liked. On 4th August 1843 he wrote 'Mr. Franklin, Bricklayer, one of the constructors, told me he would imprison any man on the works who sold me anything found there and that if he knew I asked for anything found there he would transport me if he could... I told two or three of the committee that it was not to purchase anything found there that I wished to visit it but to take notes of the character of the brickwork and anything else worthy of observation that I went but it was no use as they placed every obstacle in my way they could.' Fortunately, the window was drawn by Mr. A. J. Sprague and our intrepid clockmaker managed to sketch the doorway. Thanks to these records, the Moot Hall can now be

Restoration of a window in the Moot Hall. Drawn by A. J. Sprague in 1843.

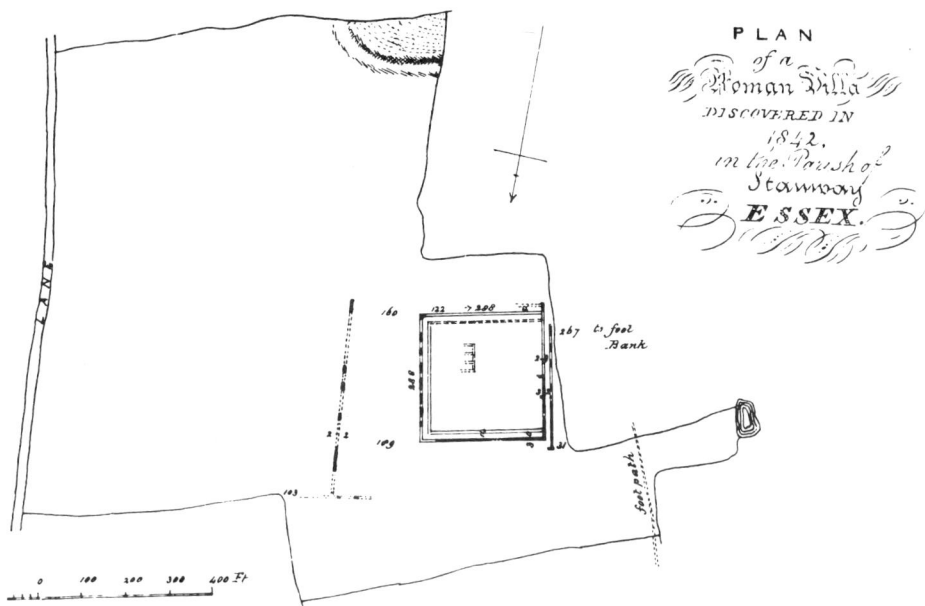

PLAN
of a
Roman Villa
DISCOVERED IN
1842.
in the Parish of
Stanway
ESSEX.

Gilbert's plan of the Reverend Jenkins's excavations at Gosbecks.

dated to *c.* 1160 and seen as the most elaborate building of its type and period known in the country.

Wire passionately believed that Colchester should have its own public museum and actively canvassed towards this end. However, partly because of his political and religious beliefs (he was both a Whig and a nonconformist), he was never in favour with the people of influence in the town and his overtures had little effect. In desperation, Wire decided to set up a private museum in his shop in the High Street and, to promote this, had a hand-bill printed in 1840 appealing for exhibits. But his scheme was short-lived because very soon poverty forced him to sell his cherished collection. Nevertheless he did not forsake archaeology and up to two weeks before his death was busy about the town writing in his notebooks and buying finds where he could. Twice bankrupted and dogged by family illness, Wire had difficult personal problems but he did have the limited satisfaction of seeing in 1846 the set-ting aside in the new Town Hall of a small room for the storage of antiquities until such time as a public museum could be founded.

It can be no coincidence that about this time the first archaeological excavations of any scale were taking place. These no doubt were symptomatic of the blossoming interest in Colchester's buried remains which helped precipitate the creation of the museum. Other factors such as the discovery of the 'Colchester Sphinx' in 1821 were to play their part too. The finding of the Sphinx during the construction of the Essex County Hospital had caused great public interest and the sculpture was to take pride of place in the new museum not long after it eventually opened some years later.

The first extensive excavations in Colchester took place in 1842 at Gosbecks near Shrub End, three miles south-west of the town centre but within the earthworks described by Morant and others. Here the Reverend Henry Jenkins dug several long trenches and uncovered walls which he believed to be part of a Roman villa but which, as we shall see, many years later proved to be a Roman temple.

The first large archaeological dig within the town walls was undertaken by Dr. P. M. Duncan in the Hollytrees Meadow in 1852. There was great excitement when a Roman drain large enough for a man to crawl along was discovered and emptied for a distance of over 200 yards. At its north end was found a small Roman gate, known since as Duncan's Gate, and at its south end lay a small building taken to be a Roman bath because of the spring which rose inside it.

In 1865 Josiah Parish, working on the site now occupied by the Gilberd

The drain in Hollytrees Meadow as exposed by Duncan in 1852. Drawing by J. Parish. (Courtesy of the Essex Archaeological Society.)

The Colchester Sphinx.

School, was the first to carry out an excavation of a private Roman house in Colchester. His method was simply to dig down to the walls and follow them, opening out only where pavements were spotted. Although by modern standards the work was very superficial, the recording of it was good compared with that of other 19th-century excavations in the town.

Possibly the first substantial local collection of antiquities was made by Mr. Charles Gray as far back as the first part of the 18th century. This collection he housed in Colchester Castle which he had acquired and partly restored. Another important collection was that of the Colchester Philosophical Society, founded in 1820. Although something of its contents is known, the collection seems to have been destroyed by fire in 1835.

Three years after the death of William Wire, the antiquities gathered in

8

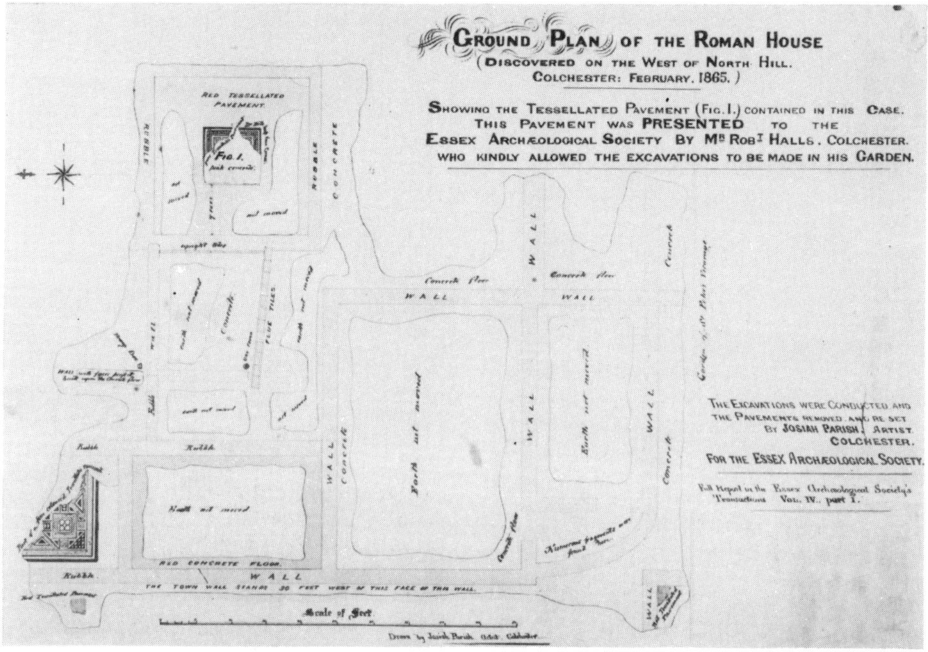

GROUND PLAN OF THE ROMAN HOUSE
(DISCOVERED ON THE WEST OF NORTH HILL.
COLCHESTER: FEBRUARY. 1865.)

SHOWING THE TESSELLATED PAVEMENT (FIG. I.) CONTAINED IN THIS CASE.
THIS PAVEMENT WAS PRESENTED TO THE
ESSEX ARCHÆOLOGICAL SOCIETY BY Mᴿ ROBᵀ HALLS. COLCHESTER.
WHO KINDLY ALLOWED THE EXCAVATIONS TO BE MADE IN HIS GARDEN.

the Town Hall were transferred to the crypt of the castle where, in September 1860, under the joint management of the Corporation and the Essex Archaeological Society, the Colchester and Essex Museum was at last opened. The provision of a proper public museum, although half-heartedly mooted for years beforehand, was finally brought to reality mainly through the efforts of the Essex Archaeological Society founded in 1852 with this as a primary objective.

By the end of the century, the museum could claim to house the largest collection of Romano-British antiquities outside London. The backbone of the collection was the contents of the private museum of George Joslin, a wealthy local business man whose antiquities were bought in 1893 following a successful public appeal for funds. Joslin and before him another keen antiquarian, John Taylor, had both lived off Lexden Road and had excavated large areas of their extensive properties in search of pots

Above: **Josiah Parish's plan of his excavation on the site of the Gilberd School. (Courtesy of the Colchester and Essex Museum.)** *Below:* **The Colchester Vase, a pot made in Colchester showing scenes of gladiatorial combat and hunting.**

The tombstone of Marcus Favonius Facilis, a centurion of the Twentieth Legion.

and other objects buried in the Roman cemetery there. Taylor started in 1848 and dug up several acres of land, unearthing 170 or more pots, the most spectacular being the so-called 'Colchester Vase'. Joslin went one step further and bought land just to dig it up; the result was that he amassed what was claimed to be the largest private collection of its kind in Britain. When catalogued in 1888, his museum contained over 800 pots and about 2,000 other objects, the most outstanding of which was a superb military tombstone erected in honour of Marcus Favonius Facilis, a centurion of the Twentieth Legion.

It has long been recognised that, for an excavation to be more than merely a search for objects for their own sake, detailed plans and notes are essential and, furthermore, that when objects are found in groups (e.g. in a grave-group, a pit or a layer), the associations should be carefully recorded. Unfortunately Taylor and Joslin appear to have kept few records of their excavations and many of the surviving so-called groups are clearly suspect. However a few are slightly better documented than others because drawings were made supposedly showing how they lay in the ground.

In addition to the material amassed by Taylor and Joslin, various other collections were either bought by the museum or acquired as gifts throughout the second half of the 19th century. These include the Acton Collection (which contained many objects recovered by Wire), the Vint Collection of bronzes from Colchester

Above: **Demolition of the Norman stone house near Jacklin's cafe in 1886. Photograph by J.C. Shenstone. (Courtesy of the Colchester and Essex Museum.)**

Below: **A drawing by Parish of one of Taylor's grave groups. (Courtesy of the Colchester and Essex Museum.)**

and abroad, and the Jarmin Collection of grave-groups.

The last decades of the 19th century were relatively quiet in archaeological terms. Of note was Joslin's discovery of some pottery kilns at Sheepen; one of these was preserved for the town in a specially-made brick building which survived until a few years ago.

In 1886, a substantial Norman stone building was demolished. It had stood in the High Street near Jacklin's shop and was at least the third stone building of this date to have been knocked down in Colchester. (The Moot Hall had been demolished in 1843 and a stone house on the west corner of Pelham's Lane had been taken down in 1730.) Fortunately during the demolition works of 1886, not only were some plans made of the building but also a series of photographs were taken. Here, probably for the first time in Colchester, the camera made a real impact as a tool for recording threatened buildings and archaeological sites.

Whilst eating his lunch in the Castle Park during the drought of 1906, the museum curator, Mr. A. G. Wright, noticed parch marks and cracks in the turf. He carried out a small investigation and found that these were caused by walls of a Roman building. Eventually, under the direction of Dr. R. E. M. Wheeler (later Sir Mortimer) a large excavation took place in 1920 and the remains of Roman houses and streets were uncovered.

About this time, Wheeler and Dr. P. G. Laver, a local surgeon and keen archaeologist, put forward the startling suggestion that the so-called 'vaults' at the base of the castle were independent of the keep itself and part of the *podium* or base of a huge Roman temple of a size unparalleled in Britain. 'Could this', it was asked, 'be the Temple of Claudius built after the foundation of the Roman colony in AD 49?' Wheeler was of course to become

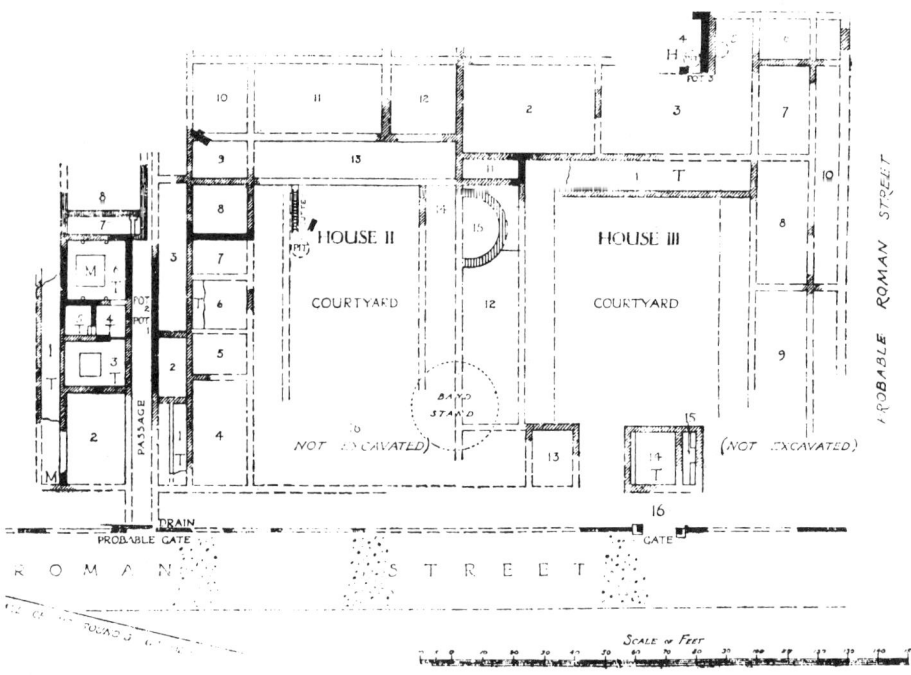

Wheeler's plan of his excavation in the Castle Park in 1920. (Courtesy of the Society of Antiquaries and the Essex Archaeological Society.)

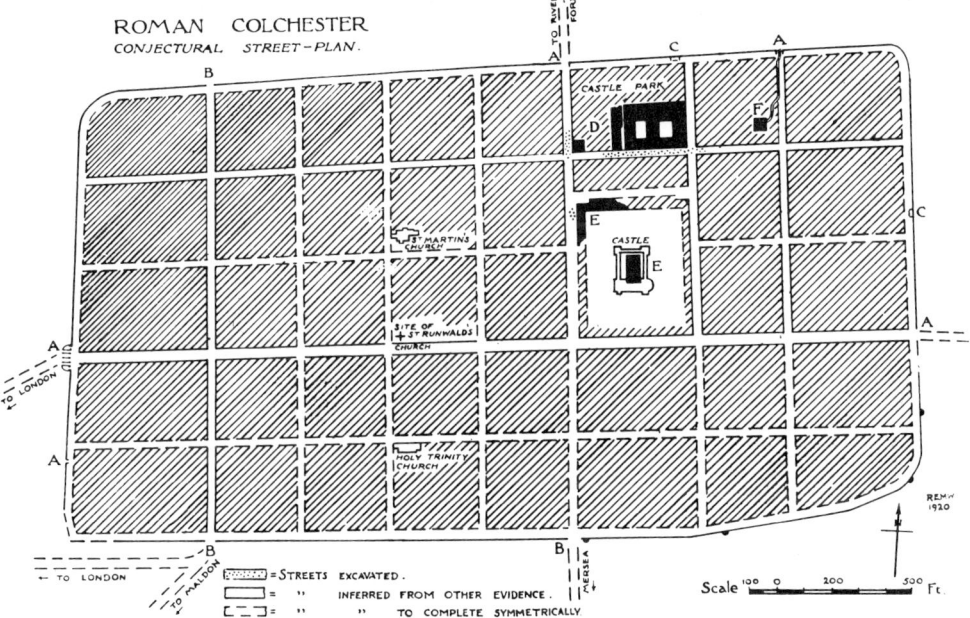

ROMAN COLCHESTER
CONJECTURAL STREET-PLAN.

= STREETS EXCAVATED.
= " INFERRED FROM OTHER EVIDENCE.
= " " TO COMPLETE SYMMETRICALLY.

Scale

The first attempted reconstruction of the street plan of the Roman town, by Wheeler in 1920. (Courtesy of the Essex Archaeological Society.)

an eminent archaeologist and well-known public figure but his first excavation was at the Balkerne Gate in Colchester where in 1917, as an army captain, he completed the work first started in 1913 by Mr. E. N. Mason and Mr. Henry Laver. He was assisted in the somewhat unorthodox excavation by two of his soldiers who tunnelled under the surviving stonework, their way lit by candle-light. One of Wheeler's most significant contributions to the study of Colchester's past was the first plan of the Roman colony in which a reconstruction of the street grid was attempted. This he did on the strength of his excavation in the Castle Park, the positions of the Roman gates (conjectural and known), and the alignment of the temple under the Castle.

The year 1926 saw the appointment of Mr. M. R. Hull as curator of the Museum and for about the next forty years, inspired by his scholarly zeal, the study of Roman and pre-Roman Col-

chester took off as never before. Numerous excavations took place about the town and, in the tradition of Wire, countless building operations were watched and discoveries carefully recorded.

The plan of Roman Colchester began to fill up: discoveries of walls, pavements, streets, and loose finds went into the records; Hull combed and correlated earlier notes and plans, back to Wire and beyond and eventually within twenty-five years of Wheeler's plan, he was able to produce a much improved version with almost all the streets of the Roman colony located and many new buildings and discoveries added. This work culminated in the publication in 1958 of his *Roman Colchester*, a volume which as an essential source of reference will remain a monument to Hull's industry for centuries to come just as Morant's history had done before him.

Philip Laver was a surgeon at the

13

Essex County Hospital and son of Henry, also a doctor. Both were much respected figures in the local archaeological circle and together they provided an invaluable ninety-year period of continuous fieldwork and support both for the Museum and the archaeology of Colchester in general. In 1924 Philip, helped by his brother, another Henry, excavated the Lexden Tumulus, a low mound in what was then Lexden Park, and as a result, the most remarkable grave-group of its period in Britain was discovered. Although apparently smashed and robbed in antiquity and consequently very incomplete, it had clearly been a magnificent group in its day. The finds included many fragments of amphorae which had originally been complete, a medallion incorporating a coin (or a copy of a coin) of Augustus, fragments of chain mail, and bronze figurines of a

The bronze boar found in the Lexden Tumulus in 1924.

boar, a bull, a griffin, and a cupid. The Lavers wisely stopped short of equating the mound with Cunobelin but did suggest that this was the burial place of a nobleman of Cunobelin's time.

Philip Laver also conducted excavations in the town centre, the largest being in Hollytrees Meadow during 1927-8. The technique employed consisted of digging trenches which were expanded at points of interest. In this way small parts of several Roman houses were uncovered to the east of the Castle and, in addition, the drain, gate, and 'bath' building discovered by Duncan were excavated more fully. In 1928, Hull took charge of operations and demonstrated that Duncan was wrong in his belief that the building at the head of the drain was a bath. Instead he suggested that it was a *mithraeum*, a temple dedicated to the god Mithras. Hull's interpretation met with considerable resistance from archaeologists in general and in 1954 he returned to the site to carry out further work in the hope of proving he was right. However, this time he found a hitherto unsuspected room in a position which effectively killed off any lingering possibility that the building might have been a *mithraeum*. It now seems more likely that the structure was a Roman waterworks.

It was in 1927 that the first evidence was recognised of the burning of the Roman town during the Boudican revolt. When Jacklin's cafe was being built, large quantities of broken burnt pottery and melted glass vessels were found which had been stored in stacks apparently as part of the stock of a

The excavation of the *'mithraeum'* in 1929. Photograph by Cosser. (Courtesy of the Colchester and Essex Museum.)

shop. The pottery consisted mostly of *terra sigillata*, an imported ware which is closely datable. The types present pointed to the conclusion that the destruction was the work of Boudica and her followers. A similar discovery was made about twenty years later on the south side of the High Street at Curry's.

The thirties saw a period of great archaeological activity. Amongst other projects, the decade witnessed the excavation of the chapel and other buildings now exposed to view on the south side of the castle, several trenches to examine the town defences, and some work at Gosbecks. In 1932 aerial photography made its first contribution to the study of Colchester's past. Photographs of Gosbecks taken by the R.A.F. during the summer of that year showed clearly that the building Jen-

kins had trenched ninety years before was not a Roman villa as he had thought but a temple within a large elaborate precinct. Buried archaeological features such as pits, ditches, and walls affect the rate at which crops directly above grow and ripen, especially during a drought. Under the right conditions these can be seen as marks in the fields. The temple at Gosbecks is of a distinctive Romano-Celtic type which in plan consists of one square placed symmetrically within another. The building occupied the corner of a large courtyard enclosed on all four sides by what was probably an elaborate double ambulatory or corridor.

But the chief excitement of the 1930s was the excavation at Sheepen which, because of the discoveries being made there, was hailed as the site of Cunobelin's capital, the very

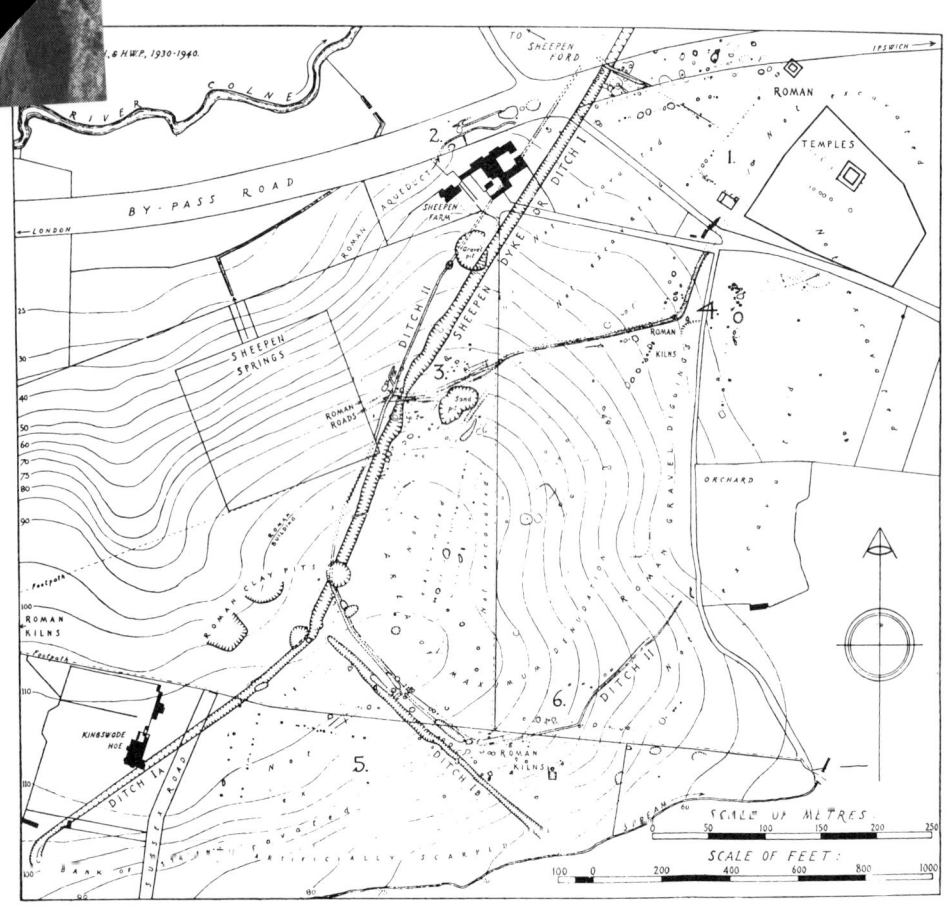

Hawkes's and Hull's plan of the Sheepen excavations of the 1930s. (Courtesy of the Society of Antiquaries.)

Camulodunum which appears on his coins. Sheepen lies about half a mile west of the town centre and its full archaeological potential was first recognised by Hull in 1928, following extensive discoveries in a gravel pit monitored by his assistant, Mr. E. J. Rudsdale. In the winter of 1929-30, the proposal to build a by-pass (now the A604) immediately north of Sheepen Farm led on the initiative of Hull and Laver to the Society of Antiquaries in London setting up an excavation committee to deal with the necessary archaeological work. Consequently in 1930, C. F. C. Hawkes (then at the British Museum) and J. N. L. Myres with members of the Oxford University Archaeological Society proceeded to excavate along the site of the by-pass whilst Hull dug south of Sheepen Lane. In 1931 and 1932, Hawkes continued his work further south and from 1933 until 1939, when the excavations ended, the rest was undertaken solely by Hull. It had been expected that all of the area would be built over although this never happened because of the advent of World War II. Thus, what had started as a 'rescue' operation soon became a major archaeological affair matching at first the

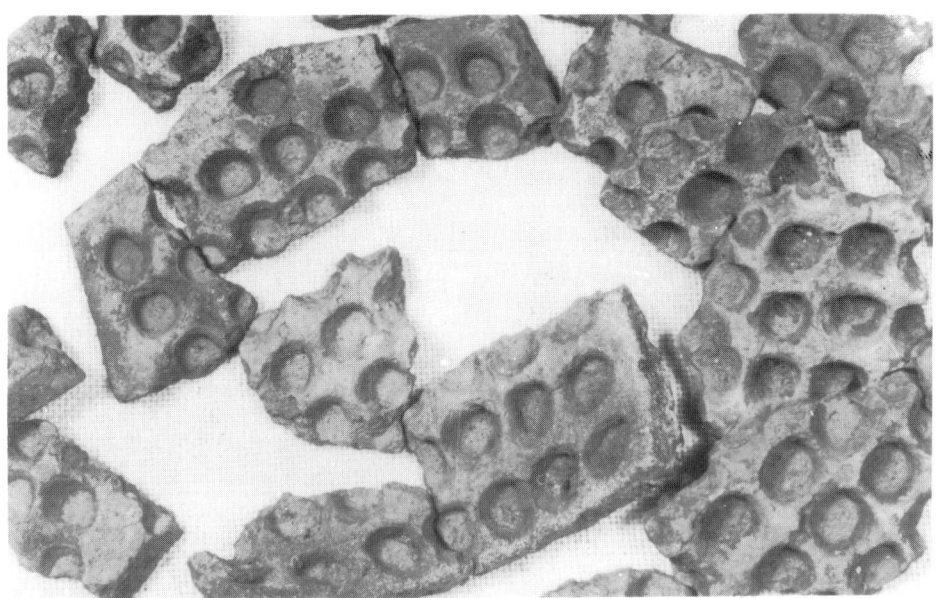

Coin 'moulds' from the Sheepen site. (These examplee were found during a small excavation in 1971.)

Verulamium excavations (1930-3) by Mortimer Wheeler and then his work at the important hillfort of Maiden Castle in Dorset. The discoveries at Sheepen included native huts, a road, a large back-filled defensive ditch (the 'Sheepen Dyke'), two Romano-Celtic temples, many pottery kilns, scores of pits, and tons of pottery and other loose finds including hundreds of coins of Cunobelin. Of dramatic significance was the discovery of many fragments of so-called coin 'moulds', indicating that here had probably been Cunobelin's mint. Each mould consisted of a slab of clay with fifty small circular flat-bottomed depressions. Molten metal would have been poured into each of these to form blanks. When cool these were removed and stamped with a die to produce the finished product.

Hull worked tirelessly at processing the pottery and other finds (some 40 tons in all); the museum had obtained for this the use of the empty Mumford's engineering works in Culver Street. The report which he wrote with C. F. C. Hawkes was delayed by the war but appeared in 1947, matching in quality the site itself and remaining a key work of reference in British archaeology. Hawkes and Hull concluded that the main period of activity at Sheepen started c. AD 10 and finished AD 60-1 when the site was sacked during the Boudican revolt. The temples and nearly all the kilns were later.

Thus the sequence of events passed down to us by Roman writers was beginning to show through in the archaeological discoveries. Colchester after all was the site of Camulodunum and the seat of Cunobelin. A Roman colony had been founded here, the remains of which lay under the modern town. A huge classical-style temple had been built at Colchester and the colony had been destroyed by fire. Not only had destruction layers of an early period been found at the native settlement at Sheepen but in the colony too, notably at the 'pottery shop' at Jacklin's.

17

The Gosbecks Mercury.

But what of the fortress of the Twentieth Legion, supposedly built here not long after the start of the invasion? Hawkes and Hull and others before them were well aware of the two superb early tombstones from Colchester. Both stones had been found near the east end of Lexden Road close to the Royal Grammar School and both may have marked the graves of men who may have died on active service. The men concerned were Facilis, a centurion of the Twentieth Legion, and Longinus, a cavalry officer of an auxiliary unit. Moreover, a master at the Royal Grammar School, Mr. A. F. Hall, had for many years carried out excavations in the vicinity of his school where he found a deep ditch and a network of Roman roads radiating from one small area. Hawkes and Hull wondered if an early military base was to be found here, south-west of the site of the later colony near the roads, ditch and tombstones. But the answer to this problem was not to be forthcoming for several decades yet.

Although World War II slowed down the pace of archaeological research in the town, it also presented new opportunities; the digging of air-raid shelters provided peepholes into the buried strata which Hull and others avidly inspected and recorded and even the recovery of an unexploded bomb had its archaeological bonus. This had missed Colchester Castle by only a few feet and when dug up was found to have penetrated and cut through a hitherto unknown Roman drain!

It was during the aftermath of the

Looking for the missing arms of Mercury at Gosbecks with mine-detectors in about 1948. (Courtesy of the Colchester and Essex Museum.)

war that metal detectors first made their appearance on Colchester's archaeological sites (and in an 'official' capacity too). A few years earlier a magnificent bronze statue of Mercury had been ploughed up near the temple at Gosbecks but unfortunately its arms were missing. In an effort to find them, the field was searched without success using mine detectors.

For the next few years, Gosbecks was the scene of a few small excavations which culminated in the discovery by Hull of a Roman theatre, about 200 yards south of the temple. Thus Gosbecks was shown to be an example of a type of sanctuary common abroad but rare in Britain, where temples occur with theatres but where there is a dearth of private houses. The importance of Gosbecks was also recognised in relation to the early development of the earthworks (dykes) which surround Colchester. These had been the subject of sporadic fieldwork since the late 19th century, notably by Henry Laver and his son, Philip. They had mapped out the earthworks with more clarity than previous attempts and had discovered several new sections. From this it was recognised that the dykes formed the defences of Iron Age Camulodunum and that the complexity of the system was the result of a long period of development in which Gosbecks played a key role.

The first controlled excavation of a dyke was undertaken by Hawkes at Lexden Park in 1932 when he examined part of the Lexden Dyke. The work marked the start of a long campaign master-minded by Hawkes and Hull over a period of about thirty years, during which time they were helped by a number of people including R. J. Appleby, an army officer, Mr. A. F. Hall, the master from the Royal Grammar School, and Mr. Bryan Blake from the Museum. Each dyke was an earthen barrier consisting of a ditch up to thirteen feet deep with a high bank behind. Trenches were dug across many dykes to discover the shape and depth of the ditches, to examine the structure of the banks where these still

Imaginative reconstruction of the south side of the precinct of the Temple of Claudius. Drawing by Peter Froste.

existed, and to recover evidence of the date of their construction. In particular, junctions of two or more dykes were excavated where possible, to discover the order in which they had been built. To this day the development of the dyke system is still not fully understood but one aspect has been clear for some time, namely that the earliest dykes are the curving ones which protected Gosbecks and that it was here rather than at Sheepen that the true origin of Camulodunum lay.

Meanwhile back in the town in 1952, a fire at Kent Blaxill's premises in the High Street enabled an excavation to take place south of the castle. Hull found the remains of a large elaborate architectural screen or colonnade, built on a foundation fifteen feet wide bounding the south side of the courtyard of the Temple of Claudius. Earlier, in 1931, part of the massive foundations of a monumental gateway had been excavated by Hull about a hundred feet to the east. This formed the centre of the screen and stood due

south of the Temple so as to form an imposing entrance into the sacred precinct.

Between the war and Hull's retirement in 1963, three more temples were discovered. One was found in 1947 by Mr. A. F. Hall in the playing field of the Royal Grammar Schol. This produced two votive plaques with inscriptions indicating that the temple was almost certainly dedicated to Silvanus, a native god of the countryside. The other two temples formed a pair and were excavated in 1959-61 by Mr. Bryan Blake. These lay within a walled precinct on the south bank of the river Colne and formed part of an important sanctuary which included the temples found nearby in the 1930s.

In 1963 the Colchester Excavation Committee (now the Colchester Archaeological Trust) was revived to cope with the task of recording the buried archaeological remains of the town threatened by the many redevelopment projects then immi-

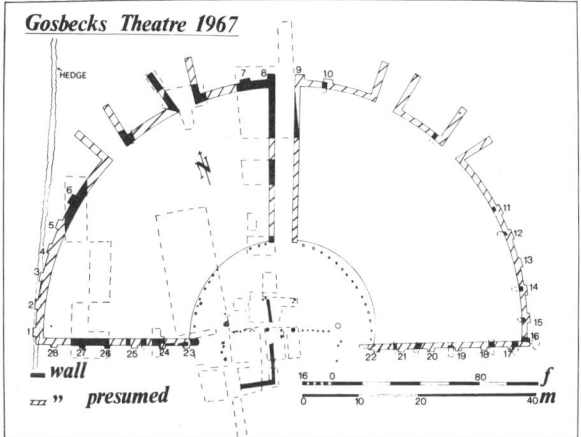

Gosbecks Theatre 1967

HEDGE

N

■ *wall*

▥ " *presumed*

Miss B. R. K. Dunnett's plan of the theatre at Gosbecks, excavated 1967. (Courtesy of Miss Dunnett and the Society for the Promotion of Roman Studies.)

nent. To direct the necessary work, Miss B. R. K. Dunnett was appointed as Colchester's first full-time director of excavations. From 1964 until 1970, Miss Dunnett conducted a series of excavations, the most significant sites being Sheepen, North Hill, the theatre at Gosbecks, and the back of the town wall by St. Mary's Rectory.

Miss Dunnett showed clearly at St. Mary's Rectory that the town wall had originally been free-standing and that its rampart was a later addition. In other Roman towns with town walls, the sequence is nearly always thought to have been the reverse.

Miss Dunnett also excavated a large part of the Gosbecks theatre and found it to have been of two periods. The theatre was originally of timber but had been rebuilt with an auditorium raised on an earthen mound. This was revetted by a large semi-circular wall interrupted for four external staircases and a central through-passage.

The excavation at North Hill in 1965 caused considerable public interest because of the discovery of three mosaic pavements, but the real importance of the site lay underneath them where Miss Dunnett found part of a building associated with early pottery. This prompted her to suspect that on North Hill lay the remains of an early Roman military base and to ask 'Could this in some way have been associated with the missing fortress of the Twentieth Legion?' Her subsequent work in the North Hill area tended to confirm her suspicions but yielded no conclusive proof. Miss Dunnett also noticed that the distribution of Claudian coins and burnt deposits of Boudican date was mostly confined to the western half of the colony suggesting that pre-Boudican Colchester was smaller than the later walled town.

Miss Dunnett's last excavation in Colchester was in 1970 at the Sheepen site and this was to be her most extensive. The work took place on part of the site which Hawkes and Hull had previously trenched in the 1930s. This time the technique of excavation was different: rather than trenching or opening up grids of small squares in the manner popular after the war, large areas were stripped and examined all in one go. The excavation confirmed earlier conclusions about the site but provided vast quantities of new finds which could be studied and assessed afresh.

SALVAGING COLCHESTER'S PAST AT LION WALK

In Colchester, the 1970s was a very exciting period from an archaeological standpoint and I was very fortunate to be able to take over the excavations at this time. The town was undergoing a series of major redevelopments as part of the town development plan and the need arose for 'rescue' excavations on a number of town-centre sites on an unprecedented scale. The task was to examine and record as much as possible of the archaeological remains before their destruction during various redevelopment projects. To meet the crisis, a full-time team was built up which, not counting site workers, consisted on average of about eight members. This included some specialists such as a draughtsman, a site planner, and a photographer and enabled a much more efficient and detailed level of work than had hitherto been possible.

To the casual observer, archaeological sites tend to look like a collection of holes and trenches dug at random, but this is not so. Each hole, trench or depression is an old feature carefully re-excavated, the contents of which are labelled with a unique identifying number and used to date it. Ideally, a site is stripped of all its features and layers by working back in time until the earliest levels are reached and removed. All layers and features are recorded and planned and their relationships and contents noted. When the excavation is over, a detailed account of the buildings and activities

Left: **Lion Walk in 1972.**

Plan of Lion Walk in the 2nd and 3rd centuries.

Large mosaic found at Lion Walk. Drawing by R. H. Moyes.

The mosaic from Lion Walk with the walking lion.

which took place on the site can be pieced together structure by structure, period by period. On urban sites such as in Colchester, the excavations can be very complex and yield vast quantities of records and finds. From 1971 to 1979, about 8,000 features such as pits, walls, and postholes have been excavated, fifteen to twenty tons of pottery and other finds recovered, and a thousand large plans drawn. And with this increase in finds, features, and records came an increase in knowledge. Over the period, excavations took place on thirty-six sites, the largest and most significant of which were at Lion Walk from 1971 to 1974 and at Balkerne Lane from 1973 to 1976.

At Lion Walk substantial parts of two Roman houses were excavated. Both were of the courtyard type having been built around a central court or garden. Since there is no local building material in Colchester, it was common practice especially in early medieval times to quarry into the buried remains of the Roman town to find stone and tile for reuse elsewhere. Thus during archaeological excavations it is frequently found that the walls and

foundations of Roman buildings have been removed or 'robbed'. Nevertheless the trenches dug to remove these can be traced and from these the plans of the buildings can be obtained. And so it was at Lion Walk.

The larger of the two houses stood next to the Roman town wall and was by Roman town-house standards very large indeed. The building had several heated rooms, a kitchen complete with ovens, and at least two mosaic pavements of 4th-century date. Both pavements were fragmentary but clearly in their day had been of a very high quality: the larger one showed a circle made up of sixteen panels of two types, narrow panels containing floral patterns and broad panels with figured scenes. At the top of the latter were inscriptions which related to the story depicted in the panels but unfortunately not enough of the pavement survived to indicate the subject-matter of the story. On the largest surviving fragment can be seen two robed figures and part of an inscription above apparently reading *AD VIA...* The other mosaic was stylistically very similar and therefore probably from the same workshop. It showed in a semi-circular

25

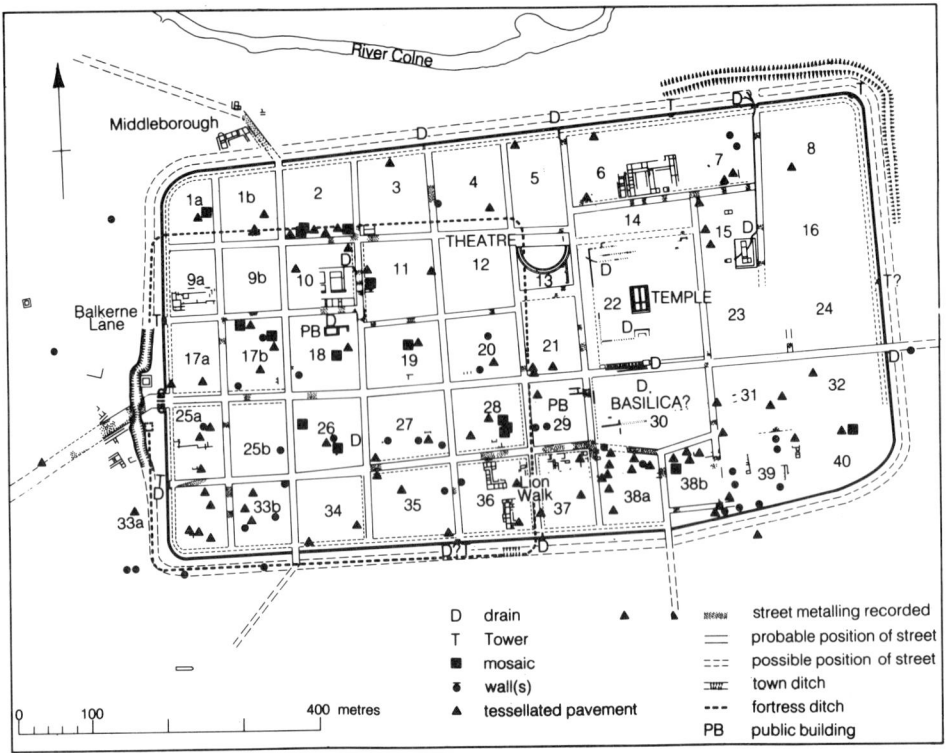

Plan of Roman Colchester *c* AD 300 showing the position of the filled-in fortress defences.

panel a lion in front of what appears to be a basket with leaves and possibly some fruit. By an extraordinary coincidence, the mosaic lay under the street Lion Walk itself. Could the street have been called after the walking lion? This is most unlikely since, other reasons apart, Lion Walk used to be called Cat Lane.

The second courtyard house, whilst not small, was of a more modest quality than the other. Not all of its floors were tessellated (*i.e.* paved with coarse red cubes), none had a mosaic pavement, and none had underfloor heating. The main domestic quarters were at the back of the premises, the front having been used for commercial purposes.

Although both buildings are of considerable interest, the most important

archaeological remains lay underneath these houses and elsewhere on the site. An unexpected yet vital discovery was of two lines of defences, one aligned north-south and the other east-west. Each consisted of a deep, V-shaped ditch with a carefully constructed rampart behind. The latter was a bank of sand, laid over a foundation of parallel timbers and revetted on both sides with walls of clay (technically sandy clay). The date of the defences was clear because, after the north-south ditch had been filled in, a street had been laid on top as part of the street grid of the colony. The buildings alongside this new street had been destroyed in AD 60-1 indicating that these defences must *predate* this event. (See plan on p 76.)

To the west of the north-south

defences was a narrow north-south street. Along the west side of the latter were the ends of six narrow buildings set so that the central four lay as two pairs back to back. This arrangement in groups of six is characteristic of barrack blocks in military fortresses and the Lion Walk buildings themselves resemble the officers' quarters found at the ends of barrack blocks.

Thus the various factors, *i.e.* the presence of early defences, the arrangement and number of the buildings, and their relationship to the street and defences to the east, all point to an early military establishment of some size. Could this at last, we wondered, be the missing fortress of the Twentieth Legion? But one important fact emerged, namely that some of our presumed military buildings had been destroyed in AD 60-1, ten years or so *after* the foundation of the town. How could this be? The implication here must be that these had survived the changeover from fortress to colony.

It had been noticed that the early buildings and defences were on a slightly different alignment to the later streets and houses including the north-south street over the filled-in ditch. The difference was only a matter of a few degrees but it was real enough and this prompted an attempt to replan the streets of the colony from scratch. By checking and replotting every stretch of Roman street and every building, it was discovered that the two alignments at Lion Walk could be detected in the street plan itself. The streets and houses of the western side of the colony shared the same alignment as the early buildings, streets and defences at Lion Walk whereas those of the eastern part of the town, including the Temple of Claudius, were on the same alignment as the later buildings and streets at Lion Walk. This dual alignment is reflected in the town walls where the western and southern stretches share the alignment of the western part of the town's street grid and the northern and eastern stretches are on its eastern alignment.

At two places on North Hill, Miss Dunnett had found a deep east-west ditch. She was unable to date this very closely and indeed it is possible that she had found not one but two ditches close by one another. However, when the town street plan was being replotted, it was noticed that if the line of Miss Dunnett's ditch (or ditches) was projected eastwards to join the line of the north-south ditch at Lion Walk projected northwards, then the area

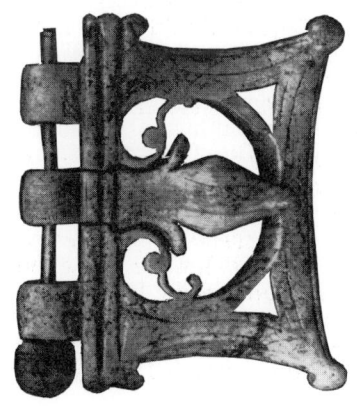

Military bone buckle from Lion Walk. Actual size.

enclosed by these two lines and the position of the town wall to the south and west is about 50 acres, a size consistent with that of known fortresses elsewhere. Also it was realized that, within this area, the spacings and positions of streets in the western half of the colony which shared the same alignment as the early buildings at Lion Walk were compatible with known plans of later fortresses elsewhere.

Thus the early sequence at Colchester seemed plain enough; we had apparently found at one stroke not only the fortress but also the mechanism whereby the new colony was established. Of all the discoveries of the 1970s, it was this that archaeologically was by far the most exciting. It would seem that rather than abandon the fortress in AD 49 when the Twentieth Legion was withdrawn, many streets and buildings were retained for use in the new colony. The defences of the fortress had been filled in and the street grid extended on the eastern side on a slightly different alignment. Within the new extension was built the Temple of Claudius. We can recall here how the Roman historian Tacitus had told us that at the time of the Boudican revolt, the town had no defences. And now at Lion Walk we can see how this came about with dramatic clarity.

The idea that the military base was taken over wholesale for civilian purposes is a revolutionary one and without a clear, known parallel anywhere in the Roman Empire outside Britain. Yet at the two other veteran colonies founded in this country, namely Gloucester and Lincoln (both slightly later

Close-up of the 2-over-2 twill from the bed burnt AD 60/1 at Lion Walk.

than Colchester), there are indications of a similar continuity. Both were on the sites of earlier legionary fortresses, both seem to have inherited and kept their legionary defences (unlike Colchester where these were demolished) and, at Gloucester at least, there is some continuity of streets, building plots, and perhaps buildings too. Furthermore Exeter and Wroxeter are other Roman towns in England where evidence is emerging of military origins for these settlements. Thus, as at Colchester, recent excavations in various places in Britain are slowly throwing light on this important and far-reaching aspect of the evolution of some of our major towns.

In many parts of the Lion Walk excavations, the destruction of the town in AD 60-1 was evident and in some places the burnt remains were

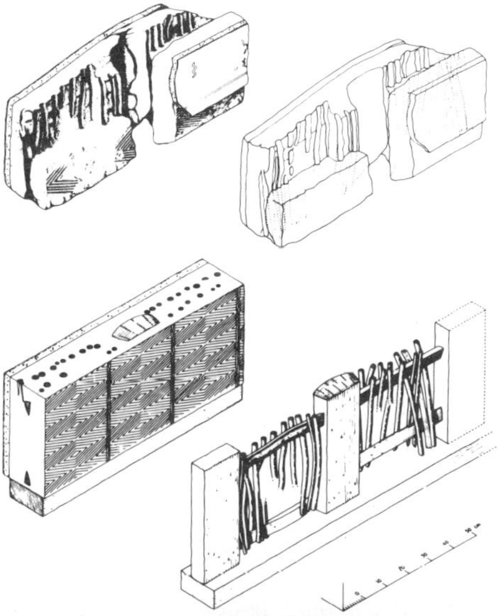

Above: **Wattle-and-daub wall at Lion Walk, burnt AD 60/1.** *Above left:* **Reconstruction of the wall showing timber frame, wattles, keyed daub, plaster and painted decoration.** *Left:* **Dates at Lion Walk, burnt AD 60/1.**

29

well preserved. Perhaps most remarkable was a charred bed in the corner of a room; this had consisted of two mattresses stuffed probably with wool and covered with woollen cloth. Although brittle, the fabric was well enough preserved to see quite clearly that it was two-over-two twill. Next to the bed was the stump of a wall still in place. Typical of many walls of this period, it consisted of a stout timber frame incorporating a horizontal baseplate. The panels between the uprights had been filled with wattles and daub and the whole structure then encased in more daub. The surfaces were keyed, plastered, and painted dark red with thin white stripes. Other objects preserved because of the fire included some dates and a plum.

A major problem in all our Romano-British towns concerns their ultimate fate. The Saxon migrations of the 5th century were closely bound up with this and at Lion Walk an important and rare contribution to our knowledge of this difficult period came in the form of two Saxon sunken huts. By comparison with Roman houses, these structures appear primitive indeed but are typical of those in early rural Saxon settlements in Britain where they can occur in large numbers. One of the Lion Walk huts belongs probably to the mid 5th century and was built close to the east-west Roman street. Characteristically it had a stout post at

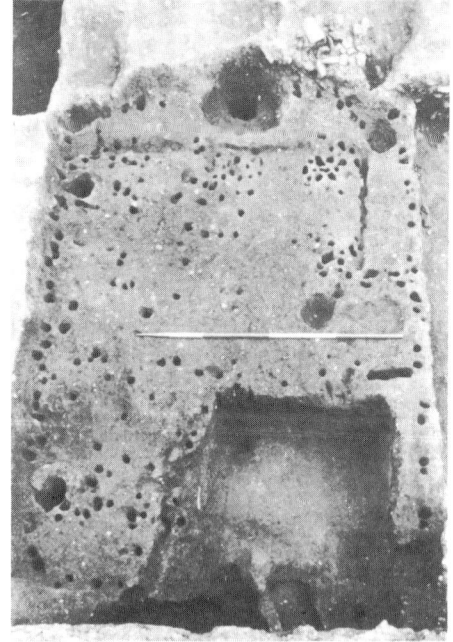

Above right: **The oval sunken area of the 5th-century hut at Lion Walk being planned.** *Right:* **The 6th- to 7th-century hut at Lion Walk.**

30

either end to support its ridge pole and also had a wooden floor over an irregularly-shaped sunken area. The second hut was larger and unusual in many respects. It appears to have been built against the outer wall of one of our two courtyard houses and its sunken floor had been dug through a stoke-hole for a hypocaust. The stoke-hole had been choked with broken tiles and mortar which had fallen from the roof of the Roman house. This conjures up a colourful image of the Anglo-Saxon hut built up against a derelict Roman house with its walls still standing but its roof caved in. Unlike the other hut, this building had no timber floor and its sunken area was peppered with stake holes. Pottery dates the hut to the 6th or 7th century and a loomweight and spindlewhorl suggest that it was used as a weaving shed. The stake holes around the edge of the sunken floor probably belong to the superstructure of the hut but those in the middle may have been associated with looms. Together the two huts seem to indicate that by *c.* AD 450 the Romano-British way of life had broken down in Colchester and that there followed at least two centuries of

Above: **Imaginative reconstruction of the Anglo-Saxon hut at Lion Walk built up against a derelict Roman house. Drawing by Peter Froste.**

Below: **Remains of Bastion 8 found at Lion Walk in 1973.**

W
E
north-south return removed and wall repaired with brick
blocked recess
wooden floor joist of 17th-century house
roughly coursed wall of small rubble – contemporary with inserted two-centred arch below
cracks
upper face projects beyond lower by 5 cms
round-headed opening
round-headed doorway
wooden lintel
repair/blocking wall of two doorways – mainly coursed septaria in hard white chalky mortar
plaster
c17th-century doorway of reused materials
plaster on face
plaster
rebate for secondary wooden jamb
ground level at time of demolition in 1971
19th- or 20th-century doorway — access to cellar
West side of secondary doorway of reduced width. Made with yellowish mortar without shell fragments
blocking of two-centred arch partially removed
face of wall
core of N-S wall
wall made of yellowish mortar with shell fragments
original doorway
reduction of width of doorway
?inserted two-centred doorway
later frontage wall
timber jambs
0
1
2
3 metres

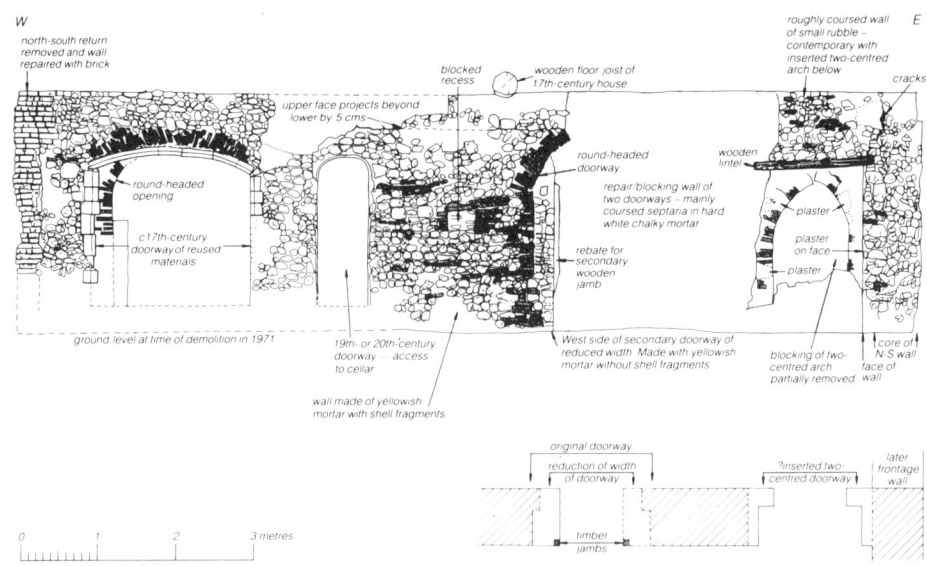

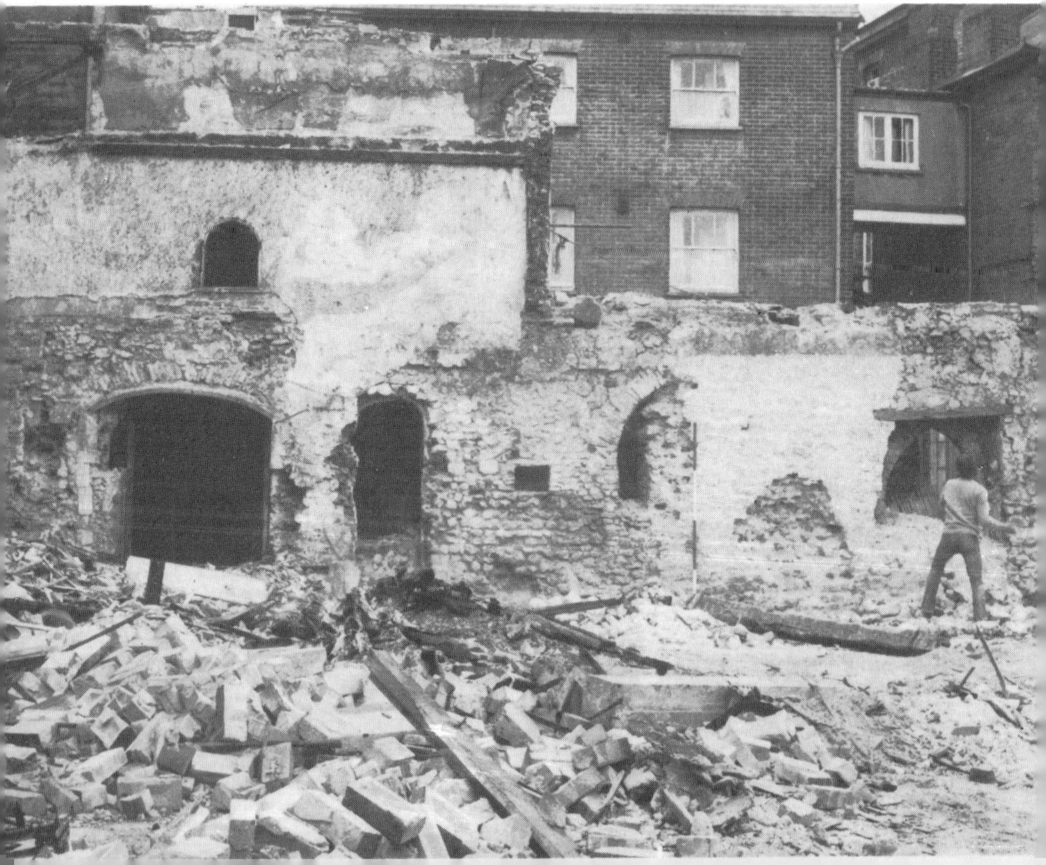

Anglo-Saxon occupation.

Other works at Lion Walk included a section behind the town wall where developers planned to breach it. Here the sequence first recognised by Miss Dunnett at St. Mary's Rectory was confirmed. The wall had been erected during the first part of the second century and the rampart added a few decades or so later. On the other side of the wall were two defensive ditches, one Roman and the other of the 11th century. Also discovered were the remains of a bastion, one of eight built c.1400 around the south-east part of the town wall circuit when the town's defences underwent extensive repairs and improvements.

At the north end of Lion Walk, a stone wall belonging to a medieval house was uncovered during the demolition of a timber-framed building. The wall, much altered, originally contained at least two doorways with semicircular heads characteristic of the later 11th and 12th centuries. Alterations included the insertion of a two-centred doorway of 13th-century date and the subsequent blocking of this and the adjacent doorway. During the excavation, the full plan of the house was recovered and the construction of the building dated to between about 1115 and 1200. This is yet another example of an early stone house in the town. Including the Moot Hall, and the two buildings in the High Street knocked down in 1730 and 1886 (p 11), there are now seven stone houses known to have existed in Colchester. Most are likely to have belonged to the 12th century and coincide with the period when quarrying into the buried Roman town was at its peak. This explains why, like the castle and the early churches of Colchester, they were built of reused Roman materials.

Below left: **Upstanding remains of the 12th-century stone house at Lion Walk.** *Above left:* **Detailed plan of the surviving wall of the house.**

BALKERNE LANE - ANOTHER CRUCIAL SITE

Before the excavations began all that was known about the Balkerne Lane site was that the main Colchester to London road crossed it obliquely and that there was a 'villa' somewhere uncovered by Dr. Henry Laver in 1876. It was hoped that if the conjectured position of the fortress as inspired by the Lion Walk excavations was correct then the western defences would be found here to help confirm this.

The ditch of the fortress was found more or less where expected although traces of its bank had been destroyed when the modern road (Balkerne Lane and Balkerne Hill) was built. Indeed it was the arrangement and sequence of defences at the Balkerne Lane site that was to be of utmost importance to our understanding not only of the site but also the development of Colchester as a whole. On the basis of these defensive changes, the sequence of occupation at Balkerne Lane can be divided into six periods. But before describing these it is necessary to look again at the Balkerne Gate, the focus of the site throughout most of Roman times.

Wheeler in 1917 had attributed the remains at the Balkerne Gate to three periods. The first period he saw as a large Roman gateway built as an integral part of the town wall and contemporary with it. This consisted of two carriageways, each flanked by a pedestrian footway, flanked in turn by an approximately quadrantal guard -room and tower. Wheeler equated the second period with a rebuilding of the two central carriageways in a different building material and the third period with the blocking of the gateway, perhaps in late Saxon times. There were several points in Wheeler's interpretation which troubled not only himself but other archaeologists. These included the unusual plan of Wheeler's first period gate and the abnormally wide carriageways this implied. Some archaeologists wondered if the gateway could somehow have been free-standing but failed to find butt-joints to prove it. However in 1974, during a re-examination of the remains, it seemed that the answer lay simply in Wheeler's interpretation; he had his first and second periods the wrong way round. Could not his Period 2 be the base of a free-standing monumental gateway with two carriageways of normal size which had subsequently been incorporated in the later town wall by the addition of flanking pedestrian footways and guardrooms? On the assumption that the original monumental gateway had been symmetrical about its north-south axis, a small hole (trench A on plan) was dug to try to locate its rear face. Although we found that the monumental gateway had been destroyed in this area, its shape, matching that at the front, was quite clear in the stonework of the wall of the pedestrian footway, and thus the new

Above right: **Wheeler's interpretation of the Balkerne Gate (courtesy of the Society of Antiquaries).** *Centre:* **Latest interpretation of the gateway.** *Bottom right:* **Trench A, looking south-east, showing the shape of the rear of the monumental gateway preserved in the later stonework.** *Bottom left:* **Two possible reconstructions of the gate.**

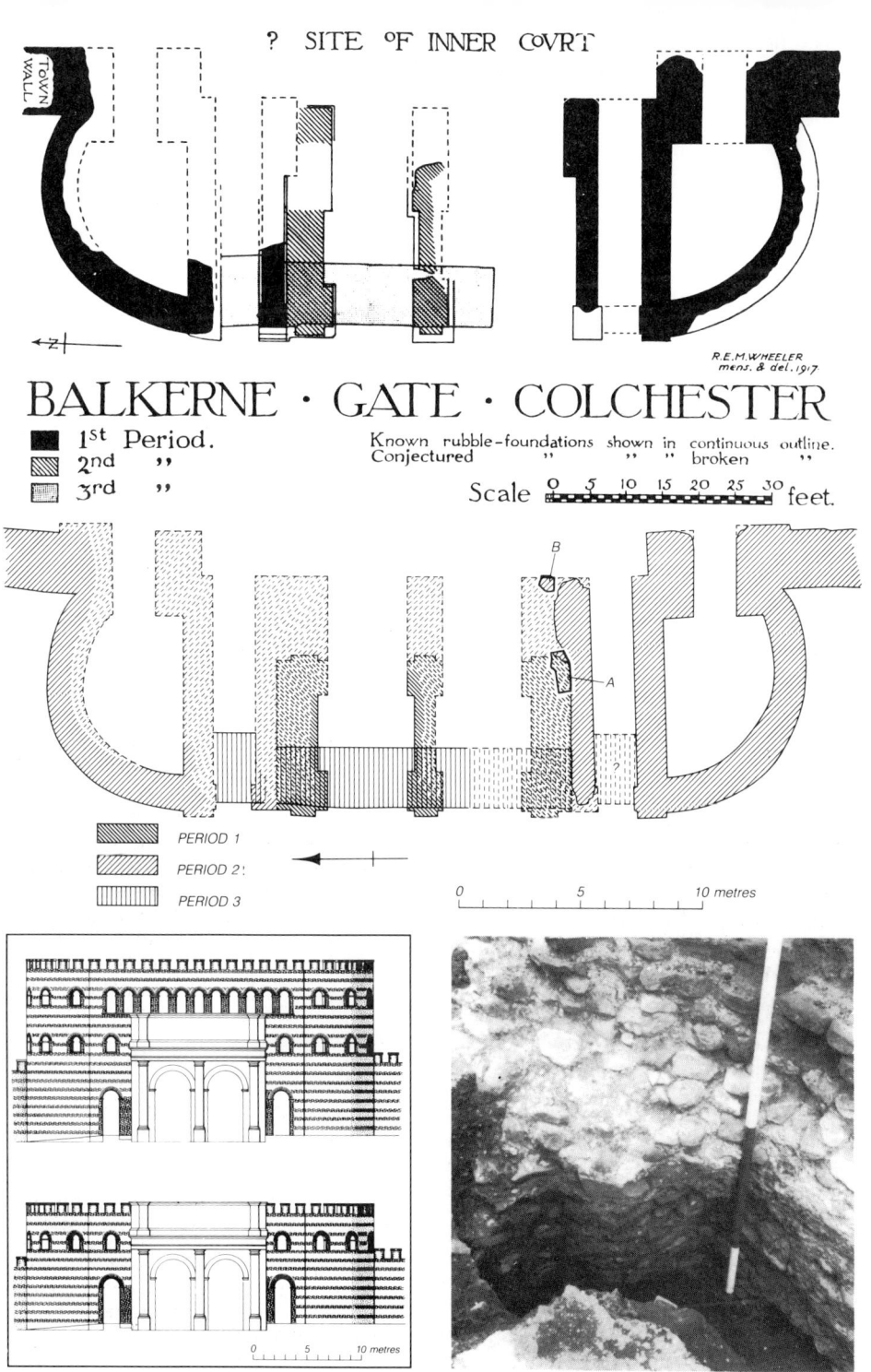

? SITE OF INNER COURT

TOWN WALL

R.E.M.WHEELER
mens. & del. 1917

BALKERNE · GATE · COLCHESTER

- ■ 1st Period.
- ▨ 2nd „
- ▦ 3rd „

Known rubble-foundations shown in continuous outline.
Conjectured „ „ „ broken „

Scale |0 5 10 15 20 25 30| feet.

B

A

?

▨ PERIOD 1
▨ PERIOD 2
▥ PERIOD 3

0 5 10 metres

0 5 10 metres

interpretation was verified. Two possible reconstructions suggest themselves for the gateway in its new, second period. The larger of these is defensively the stronger and assumes a gallery over the top of the monumental gateway.

On the main excavation site opposite the gate, the first occupation (our Period 1) predates the monumental gateway and is represented by a series of small flimsy buildings set close against the London-to-Colchester road. These lay west of the legionary ditch and formed part of a civilian settlement which grew up outside the fortress.

A startling discovery came from the legionary ditch where, in the silt and debris at the bottom, lay very fragmentary remains of a minimum of six people, all of whom had probably been executed. The remains consisted of various odd bones, mainly parts of limbs, and six skulls. One of the skulls has a long cut made by a weapon such as a sword or an axe. The mark is consistent with the kind of wound which would be caused by a misdirected blow during a decapitation. Another of the skulls had a compressed fracture indicative of a blow with a 'blunt instrument'. The human remains probably found their way into the ditch by chance and were parts of what presumably had been a large number of corpses or parts of corpses left at the fortress's west gate (subsequently the site of the Balkerne Gate). The preponderance of skulls hints that it was mainly (but not exclusively) the heads of the victims which were

Above: Skull from Balkerne Lane with a long cut. *Right:* Skull from Balkerne Lane with a compressed fracture.

36

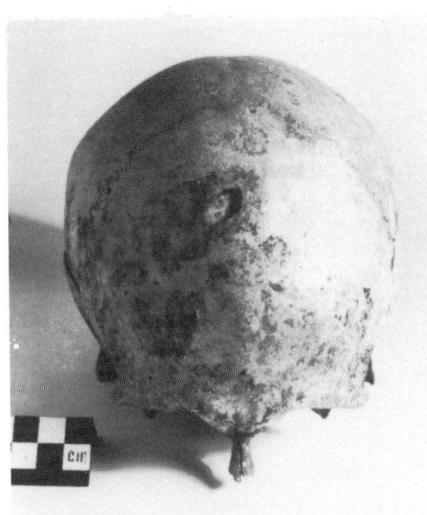

exposed to public view. It is not clear if the people had been natives or disgraced soldiers.

The second period of occupation at the Balkerne Lane site began with the levelling of the legionary defences and the founding of the Roman colony. Houses of better quality than before were built over the military ditch; these were tightly packed and extended far back from the street frontage because space was at a premium and the town was bustling with activity. The houses fronted not only the main London-to-Colchester road but also the narrow road which had formerly run along the rear of the military defences and was now retained in the new colony. Many of the houses were separated from one another by narrow gravelled alleys and several had been clearly been enlarged in a piecemeal fashion with a sequence of extensions at the rear. Most of these houses were of a lower standard of construction than the contemporary buildings at Lion Walk; their roofs were thatched, not tiled, and their walls were of a simple wattle-and-daub type in which the uprights were merely stakes hammered into the ground. Again, as at Lion Walk, the absence of defences at the time of the Boudican attack was apparent.

After the devastation of AD 60-1, the colony was provided with its first defences. These took the form of a bank and ditch which, at Balkerne Lane (now in Period 3), followed closely the course of the earlier legionary defences. The discovery of this ditch at Balkerne Lane and the close dating of it which the circumstances of

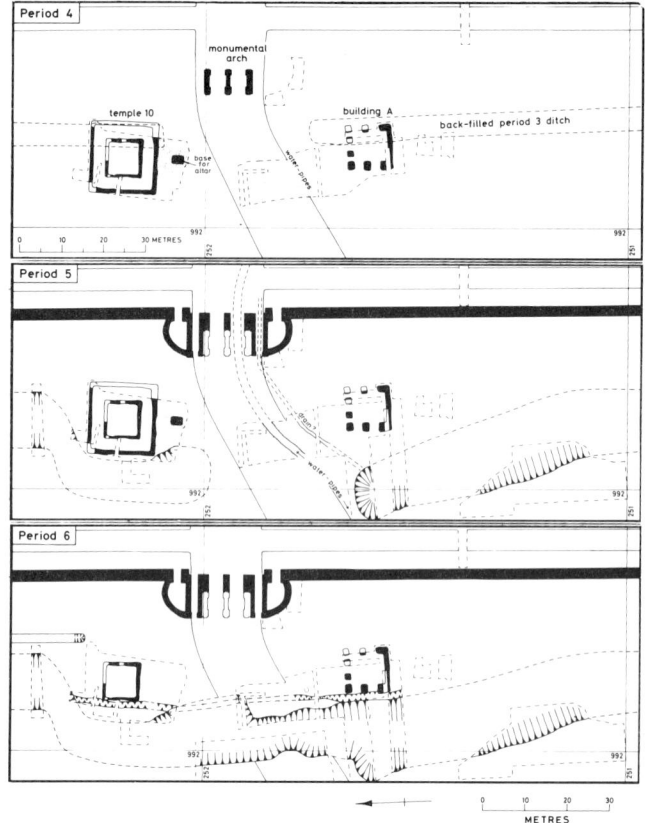

Plans of the Balkerne Lane site from the late 1st to the 4th centuries.

the site made possible introduced a new dimension to our knowledge of the town's defences.

Period 4 was a time of expansion; at Balkerne Lane the post-Boudican ditch was filled in and apparently replaced with one several hundred yards further west. On the site of the levelled defences at Balkerne Lane, three public buildings were erected; a monumental arch (Period 1 of the Balkerne Gate) and two temples. As a group they would have provided an imposing and balanced entrance into the colony proper. The arch with its two carriageways straddled the main road and had a temple on each side. The northern temple was of the standard Romano-Celtic type similar to those found at Sheepen and Gosbecks but the southern building was roughly square with three of its sides built on piers. Its foundations were built on timber piles intended to help stabilize what was presumably a top-heavy structure. Although its plan is unusual and hard to parallel closely, the building was probably a temple.

During the first part of the 2nd century, the Roman authorities decided to improve the defences of the colony by erecting a stone wall. Perhaps for reasons of expense or possibly jurisdiction, it was decided to build the wall along the line of the earlier defences at Balkerne Lane rather than incorporate the recently-defended area to the west. However there was

Imaginative reconstruction of the Balkerne Gate area *c* AD 275, viewed from the south-west. Drawing by Peter Froste.

the difficulty of what to do with the three public buildings. Were these to be demolished or could they be saved? An ingenious solution was conceived in which the new ditch that was to follow the foot of the town wall was swung around the west sides of the two temples leaving them perched between wall and ditch. Thus the three buildings were saved and Balkerne Lane moved into its fifth period.

Although the arrangement at Balkerne Lane satisfied the conservationists, it was militarily deficient. The new gateway did not have the flanking towers which projected beyond the face of the monumental gateway and were standard in gates elsewhere, nor perhaps did it have an overhead gal-

lery. Moreover the ditch was too far out from the wall and the view from the gate was obscured by the two temples. These considerations led late in the 3rd century to a strengthening of the defences by joining the butt ends of the ditch. Thus during Period 6 the Roman road was cut off and the gateway was made redundant. Although limited access across the ditch was available some time after AD 330 when the ditch had partly silted up, this nevertheless marked the end of the Balkerne Gate as the principal entrance into the colony. This explains why today the old Colchester-to-London road enters the town not by the Balkerne Gate but by the Head Gate, the *'Porta Capitalis'* or chief gate

0   1   2 metres

of medieval times, and why the High Street now stops short of the Balkerne Gate.

The changing defensive arrangements at Balkerne Lane had their effect on the private houses to the west. At first these were small and simple and belonged to a civil settlement outside the fortress but, after the foundation of the colony, they were replaced with houses of better quality Following the Boudican destruction, many of the new houses were rebuilt on the same plots as before. One of these had elaborately painted walls in which the decorative scheme probably included several scenes of gladiatorial combat.

With the building of the town wall, the area seems to have degenerated; certainly after the road through the gate was closed, the only buildings appear to have been of timber and of much lower quality than contemporary houses found elsewhere in Colchester. Eventually, probably in the 5th century, the area reverted to open land and was not substantially built on again

Above: **Conjectural reconstruction of collapsed Roman wall plaster with gladiatorial scenes. By Roger Ling. The black borders are shaded.** *Below:* **Decorative wall plaster panel showing vegetal candelabra. Probably from the same wall which contained the gladiators.** *Right:* **wall painting of a gladiator.**

black
red
buff
pink with black splashes

0   10   20 cm

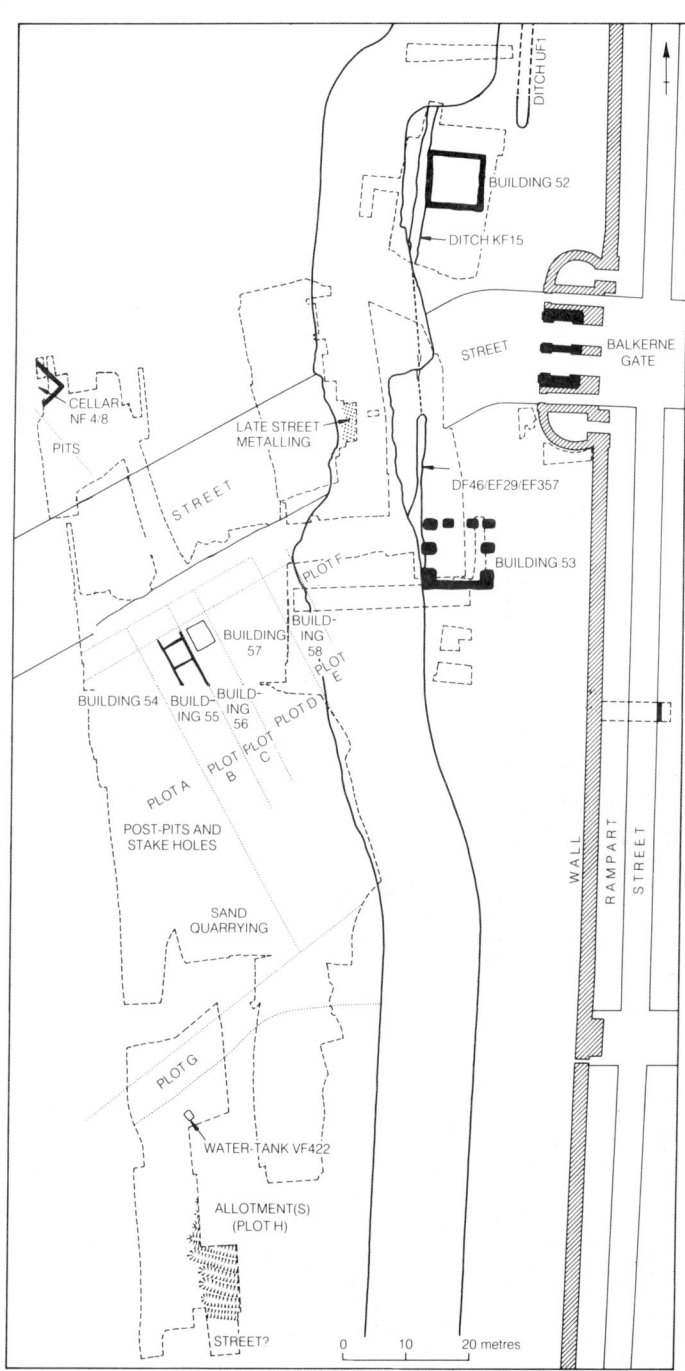

Right: **Plan of the Balkerne Lane site, Periods 5 to 6 (3rd and 4th centuries).** *Left:* **Remains of a 2nd-century house to the west of the defences at Balkerne Lane.**

43

until Victorian times.

Some information came to light at Balkerne Lane about the Roman town's water-supply. A group of four water-mains lay alongside the Roman road and isolated examples occurred elsewhere. Each main had consisted of a series of wooden pipes, each about eight feet long. These were held together by flat circular iron bands hammered into the ends of each pair of adjacent pipes to form junctions which were watertight and pressure-resistant. Identifying the probable source of the Roman town's water supply is a problem because much of the colony was about fifty feet above the natural water-table. Was the water brought from a distant source *via* an aqueduct or was it lifted or pumped uphill in some way? The roadside group of water-mains at Balkerne Lane must no doubt have led from a large water-tower, perhaps situated a little to the east of the Balkerne Gate. In themselves they throw no light on how the difficulties posed by the low water-table were overcome, but they do at least point to a plentiful supply of water in the town.

Another discovery of special interest was a Roman allotment or garden. Fortunately its surface had been perfectly preserved by the dumping over it of a thick layer of soil in the late 3rd century. In the allotment were at least nine low ridges, up to eight inches high and about seven feet apart. These were probably beds for vegetables.

Remains of four water-mains at Balkerne Lane.

EXCITING DISCOVERIES AT THE OLD CATTLE MARKET SITE

When the excavations began in 1978 on the site of the Old Cattle Market at Middleborough very little was known about the archaeology of the area. The site lies outside the walled part of the colony, between the river Colne and the town wall. It had been thought that because of Middleborough's low-lying position, the area may have been damp and marshy during the Roman period and that therefore little might be found here. However, almost as soon as work began, it became clear that the archae-ological remains were extensive.

Leading obliquely across the site from the Roman gate at the foot of North Hill was a Roman road which at its northern end turned sharply towards Sheepen, half a mile to the west. Adjacent to this were three Roman houses of 2nd- to 3rd-century date. Probably the largest of these fronted on to the west side of the

Imaginative reconstruction of the Old Cattle Market site *c* AD 200, viewed from the north. Drawing by Peter Froste.

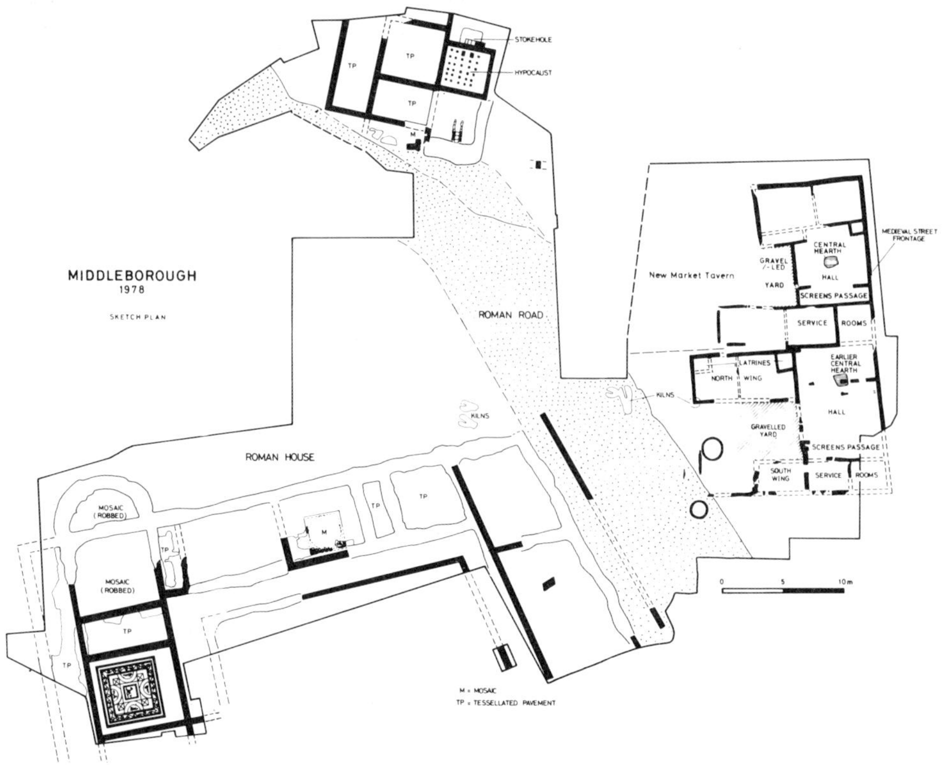

Plan of excavation (map labels):

STOKEHOLE
HYPOCAUST
MIDDLEBOROUGH
1978
SKETCH PLAN
ROMAN ROAD
MEDIEVAL STREET FRONTAGE
CENTRAL HEARTH
GRAVELLED YARD
HALL
New Market Tavern
SCREENS PASSAGE
SERVICE ROOMS
EARLIER CENTRAL HEARTH
LATRINES
NORTH WING
KILNS
HALL
GRAVELLED YARD
SCREENS PASSAGE
SOUTH WING
SERVICE ROOMS
ROMAN HOUSE
MOSAIC (ROBBED)
MOSAIC (ROBBED)
TP
M
0   5   10 m
M = MOSAIC
TP = TESSELLATED PAVEMENT

Above: **Plan of the excavation at the Old Cattle Market site showing on the left the remains of the large Roman house.**

Roman road and, despite being outside the walled area of the town, is the biggest private Roman house so far found in Colchester. Like those at Lion Walk, the house had been built around a central courtyard which it enclosed on three, if not four, sides. The front rooms had plain clay floors and presumably had been used for commercial purposes whereas the main private quarters were at the rear of the property, the largest room having an apsidal end. Of the rooms excavated, three had mosaic pavements. The smallest of these had been laid in the central room of the northern range. All that survived were two corners in each of which was depicted a cantharus, a type of vessel commonly shown on mosaics. The

Left: **A cantharus in the corner of the small mosaic from the Old Cattle Market site.** *Right:* **Excavations in progress at the Old Cattle Market site with the remains of the large Roman house in the foreground.**

46

The large mosaic from the Old Cattle Market site. Drawing by R. H. Moyes.

second pavement had been scraped up during the demolition of the house, probably around the end of the 3rd century, and the cubes no doubt salvaged for reuse elsewhere. The third pavement was of a very high quality. In Roman times it had been repaired with several large patches of unsightly pink mortar and also had been damaged by the insertion into it, left of centre, of a large circular object which was perhaps a domestic shrine. Nevertheless, the pavement was comparatively well preserved. The square central panel shows two wrestling cupids watched by a bird and is surrounded by two bands of elaborate and colourful ribbon decoration or 'guilloche'. At the centre of each side is a semicircular panel containing a sea-beast, the two intact panels showing a sea-goat and a sea-horse. The design is completed by an attractive border consisting of a foliate scroll containing in its roundels birds and two types of lotus flower and ivy leaf.

A close examination of the pavement throws light on the organisation of the firm of mosaicists employed to make it. The design of the pavement had been carefully worked out beforehand and the distribution of the two types of lotus flower and ivy leaf planned in a logical fashion. Yet a number of mistakes in the pattern were made when the pavement was laid, the worst of which was to muddle up completely the contents of the roundels down one side. Two minor errors also occur in the same row. The ivy leaf in the corner was laid as if it were in the side, *i.e.* it is at right angles to the side

Mistakes made during the laying of the large mosaic pavement at the Old Cattle Market site. The inner square shows the actual positions of the various motifs. The intended motifs are shown on the outside where these have been positioned wrongly.

not diagonally towards the centre of the pavement as it should be. Also part of its adjacent scroll was laid so that the foliage runs anti-clockwise, not clockwise as it is everywhere else. The implication in all these mistakes is that the mosaicist who laid this part of the pavement did not understand the design and therefore was not involved in its creation. Perhaps then there were two craftsmen who worked on the mosaic? The standard of workmanship across the pavement is very uniform except in one corner (bottom right-hand side) where the scroll is slightly heavier and clumsier than elsewhere. Perhaps then we can detect at least three people here?

Mrs. J. Whiffing, the museum conservator at the time, had hoped to remove the mosaic by covering it with glue and bandages and rolling it on to a long drum as if the pavement were a carpet, but the cubes proved to be too firmly set and instead the pavement had to be lifted in small flat sections. When the bedding of the mosaic was examined, it was discovered that the room originally had a plain mortar floor with a quarter-round skirting. The skirting had been smashed off and, to provide a key for the new mortar bed, the surface of the floor was pounded with a heavy tool to make dozens of little depressions. We had wondered why, when the building was demolished, the cubes of this pavement had not been salvaged along with those in the apsidal room, but the reason for this is now clear; the two pavements were of different periods and the mortar bed for the surviving mosaic was by far the tougher of the two. This

Depressions made to form a key in the mortar floor under the large mosaic pavement at the Old Cattle Market site.

explains in part why the plan to roll the pavement had to be abandoned. The museum conservator found that the mortar was too strong, just as the Roman demolition gang had done about 1700 years earlier!

Of the other two buildings on the site, only small areas could be uncovered. The largest of these was the wing of a house which lay mostly under the modern street forming the northern boundary of the site. The wing consisted of a range of rooms flanked on the west by a corridor and on the east by a pair of small heated rooms, added at a later date. The hypocaust and its stokehole were well preserved and contained pottery the date of which indicates that the house was in use after the construction of the town wall.

The large house with the mosaics had not been the first one on the site

The large mosaic pavement being lifted in sections.

Reconstruction of the lower half of a painted wall found at the Old Cattle Market site.

because underneath lay the remains of two successive buildings. In the demolition debris of the later of the two houses lay large sheets of painted wall plaster. These were lifted using plaster of Paris and bandages and enabled the reconstruction, at least on paper, of a large area of a painted Roman wall. The upper part was plain red with blank panels formed by white and green stripes. The dado was grey with long, yellow panels; below, at the base of the wall, was a narrow band of speckled pink intended to imitate marble.

In general, the excavation at Middleborough showed clearly that there had been an extensive suburb outside the town wall. The road discovered on the site provides our first known link between the Roman colony and the site of the native settlement at Sheepen. Although its course cannot be plotted accurately, the road across the Cattle Market site probably met roughly at right angles the road discovered in the 1930s across Sheepen.

Of special interest were the remains of some pottery kilns, one Roman and the rest early medieval. Colchester had been an important pottery-making centre in Roman times and the Roman kiln from the Cattle Market site is about the forty-second to be recorded in Colchester.

From the outside, the New Market Tavern appeared to date to the 19th century but this was only because it had a brick façade erected not long after the opening of the Cattle Market in the early 1860s. Inside were the timbers of a much older building. The

Kilns from the Old Cattle Market site. *Above:* Roman. *Below:* Medieval.

51

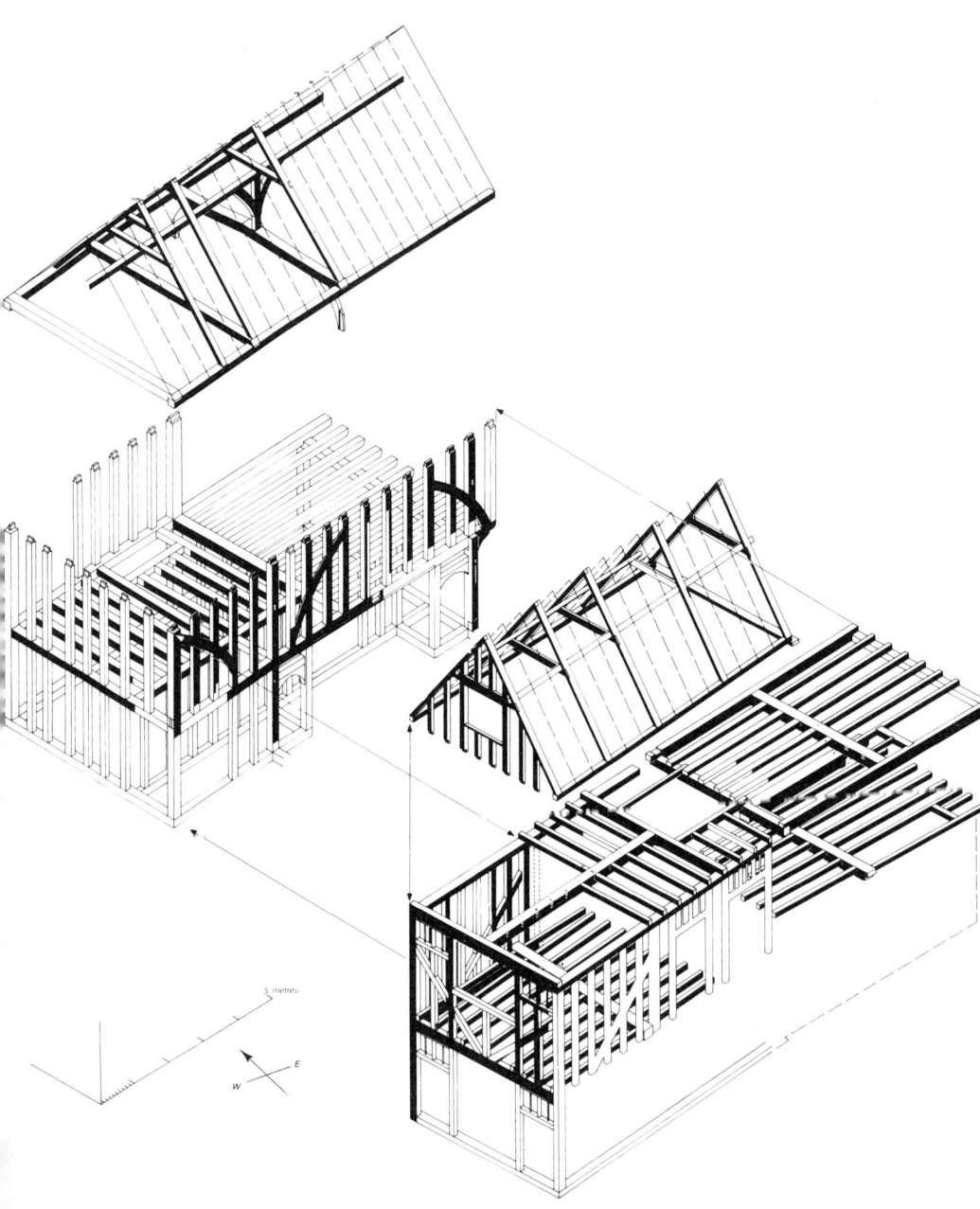

An exploded diagram showing the surviving timbers in the **New Market Tavern**. The unshaded timbers have been inferred from empty mortices.

Tavern had to be demolished as part of the redevelopment of the Cattle Market site and thus its removal provided an ideal opportunity to compare in detail the superstructure of a timber-framed house with its underlying archaeological remains.

The plan, structure, and joints of timber-framed houses evolved with time and therefore are all capable of being dated. By studying and recording the surviving timber frame of the New Market Tavern, it was clear that the structural sequence that it embodied was complex. The oldest part of the building was the cross-wing of a 15th-century hall-house, the hall or main living room of which had been demolished. Medieval halls like the New Market had to be tall to allow the smoke from their central hearths to rise and escape through a vent in the roof without causing discomfort to their occupants. The widespread use of brick chimney-stacks in the 16th and 17th centuries led to a revolutionary change in house plans. And in existing houses, a chimney-stack could be inserted into the hall which could then be divided into two by making a new floor at first-floor level. Alternatively the hall could be demolished and replaced by a new two-storey block. At the New Market Tavern, both methods were used. First the hall was divided into two and a chimney-stack inserted. But then, in the 17th century, it was demolished and replaced with a slightly taller two-storey block which afforded greater head-room than before. Other structural changes to the house included a late 17th-century addition of a two-storey extension to the rear of the hall-block.

Fortunately the New Market Tavern had no cellars and the archaeological remains were well preserved. Amongst other discoveries were the central hearth and the base of the early brick chimney-stack. The remains were also discovered of earlier phases of the house dating back to about the 14th century so that a long sequence was obtained spanning six centuries or so.

The adjacent property to the south was also excavated. Although no above-ground structure survived there, the archaeological remains matched closely in plan and construction those of the New Market Tavern itself.

Thus the excavations at the Cattle Market uncovered a wealth of information about what had been a thriving area of both Roman and medieval Colchester.

The New Market Tavern.

MORE DISCOVERIES OF THE 1970S

Although the bulk of the Museum's Roman collection has come from the town's cemeteries, until the 1970s surprisingly little controlled excavation had taken place in these areas. In 1934-42, Mr. A. F. Hall excavated a small 'walled cemetery' in the grounds of the Royal Grammar School and at about the same time a small group of inhumations were uncovered at the Sheepen site. In 1971-2, two more small areas were excavated, each yielding about twenty Roman burials, one site being near the Maldon Road and the other overlooking St. Botolph's roundabout. However, easily the most important cemetery excavation was at Butt Road where, between 1976 and 1979, nearly seven hundred skeletons were examined. Most of these were laid east-west and belonged to a 4th-century cemetery. Nearly all the other burials were aligned north-south and formed part of a cemetery which dated to the 3rd and early 4th centuries and lay under part of the later one. Most of the skeletons were in nailed wooden coffins but various other burial types were evident. These included lead coffins, hollowed tree trunks, graves with no coffins at all, and timber vaults. Some of the burials were accompanied by objects such as pots, footwear, armlets, necklaces, and hairpins. Although these occurred in both cemeteries, objects were placed less frequently in the east-west burials. Exceptional were four beautiful glass vessels shared between three graves close by one another.

The value of excavating such a large number of skeletons lies not only in the opportunity to examine the structure and organisation of a Roman cemetery but also in the chance to inspect the skeletal remains of a large sample of the population of late Roman Colchester. From the bones, specialists can tell much about details such as sex, build, diet, disease, age at death, and racial characteristics and, by studying a large number of skeletons, they can generalise with greater confidence on the various physical attributes of the contemporary population as a whole.

Next to the cemetery stood a long building with an apsidal eastern end. The building had been partly examined

SAND PIT

0   10   20 metres

Plan of burials and possible Roman church at Butt Road.

Above: **Glass vessels found at Butt Road.**
Right: **Two of the vessels in place at the foot of a burial.**

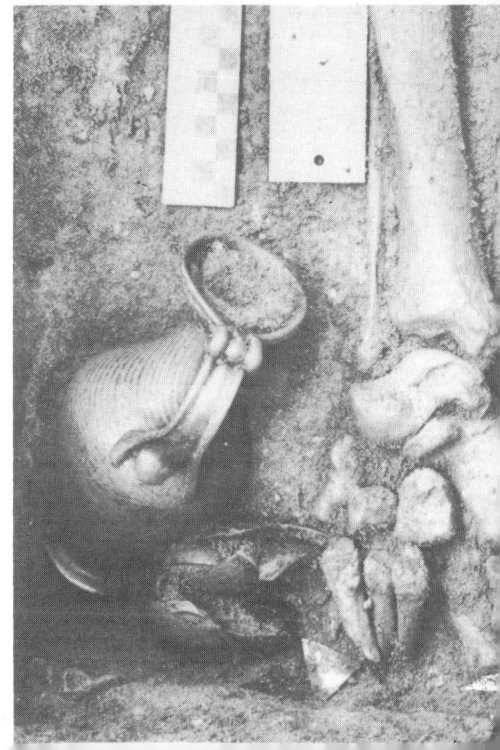

by Hull and later Miss Dunnett but, during the Butt Road excavations, it proved possible to uncover the remains almost completely. Although very badly damaged by relatively recent activities, the eastern end of the building appeared to have been aisled, the evidence for which is provided by two possible rows of post-pits aligned on the northern and southern ends of the apse. Also at the east end were some grave-like features which, although without bones, suggest that this may have been a '*martyrium*', a cemetery church built around the burial of an important Christian. Finds from the site, especially coins, point to activity starting *c.* AD 320-40 and continuing into the 5th century. The various features of the building, namely the plan, the grave-like features, its

Plan of possible Roman church at Butt Road. The main areas destroyed by later pits and trenches are shown grey.

period of use, and the adjacent late Roman cemetery are all consistent with, if not in themselves diagnostic of, a Roman cemetery church. But unfortunately conclusive proof of this is absent.

Of all the smaller excavations which took place during the 1970s, perhaps the most interesting was in the grounds of St. John's Abbey near St. Botolph's Roundabout. Here were found the remains of an Anglo-Saxon church which documentary sources indicate was dedicated to St. John the Evangelist and was probably demolished in 1095 when St. John's Abbey was founded. Its plan was unusual and likely to have been of two periods. At first the church seems to have been of the rare 'tower-nave' type, when it consisted of an apsidal chancel to the east and a tall square nave founded on deeper foundations; later the church appears to have been enlarged with the addition of a new nave to the west. The building was substantially of reused Roman materials, and built (by chance) on the site of a Roman cemetery. After the demolition of the church, the area was used as a burial ground for the Abbey.

Despite great archaeological activity in the town centre in the 1970s, the massive system of earthworks concentrated on the west side of Colchester and the native occupation associated with it were not neglected. Of special interest was a trench in 1977 dug across Gryme's Dyke, the westernmost of the earthworks. At the base of its bank lay a sherd of samian and a coin of Claudius, each indicating independently that the dyke was constructed *after* the Roman conquest. In the 1950s, Professor Hawkes sectioned the Triple Dyke (just to the east of Gryme's Dyke) and had suggested that it was Roman, a conclusion now matched by the discovery at Gryme's Dyke. For a long time, the dyke system had been equated exclusively with the defences of pre-Roman Camulodunum and regarded as having had a long period of development. However we can now see that after AD 43 not only was the system maintained but, surprisingly, it appears to have been enlarged.

In the 18th century, Stukeley had guessed that the oval hillfort at West Bergholt (Pitchbury Ramparts) was the 'British Oppidum', *i.e.* the site of Camulodunum itself, and had shown it as such in his drawings (p 4). Later Hawkes and Hull had instead wondered if the hillfort had simply been the

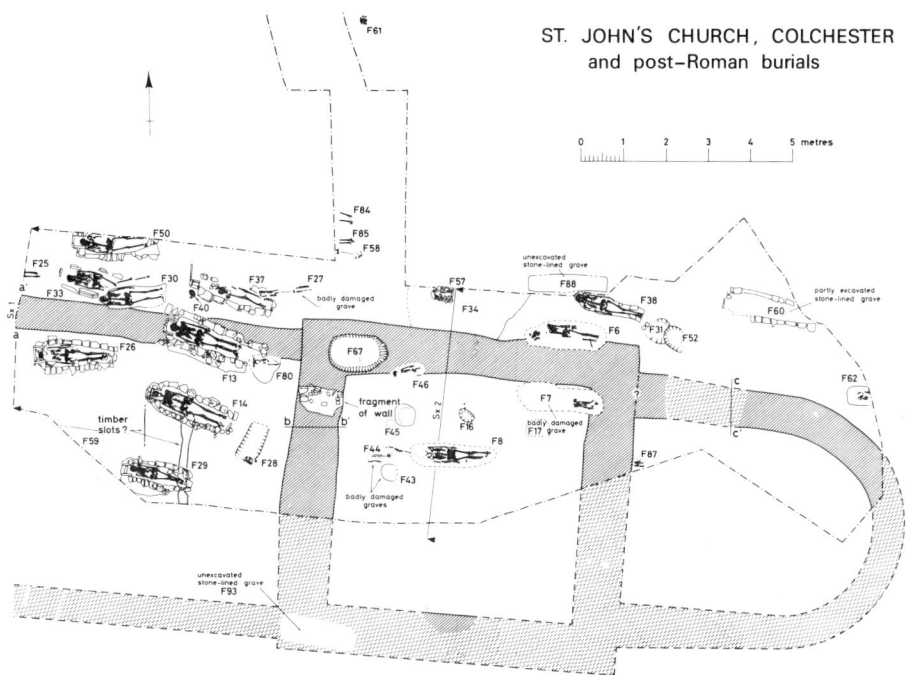

ST. JOHN'S CHURCH, COLCHESTER
and post-Roman burials

Plan of St. John's, the Anglo-Saxon church near St. Botolph's Roundabout.

modest forerunner of the huge dyke system to the south. Excavations were carried out on the site in 1933 and again in 1973. On neither occasion were the results conclusive but charcoal found under the rampart in 1973 was dated by radiocarbon analysis to the 6th-4th centuries BC. Thus Pitchbury may have been centuries earlier than hitherto thought and therefore may have had little bearing on the origin and development of Camulodunum. However, more excavations are required to resolve the problem.

The dry summers of the mid 1970s produced spectacular cropmarks throughout Britain and at Gosbecks the buried archaeological features could be detected as never before. Hundreds of aerial photographs of the area were taken and this enabled a detailed plan of Gosbecks to be made. Although the coverage is far from complete, so good and clear were many of the photographs that the nature and layout of Gosbecks in the late Iron Age and early Roman periods have been made plain.

The focus of the settlement was a large subrectangular enclosure within which would have been the earliest houses, perhaps even the royal household of the Trinovantes. Leading from the west corner of this was a complex system of ditched trackways and fields. Although concentrated between the subrectangular enclosure and the dykes to the west, the trackways formed part of an intricate web which reached out for miles around and in effect were the roads of Camulodunum itself. But they were not roads in the modern sense; they were not metalled, had no footways and, being ditched on either side, were principally droveways for farm animals. The settlement was essentially

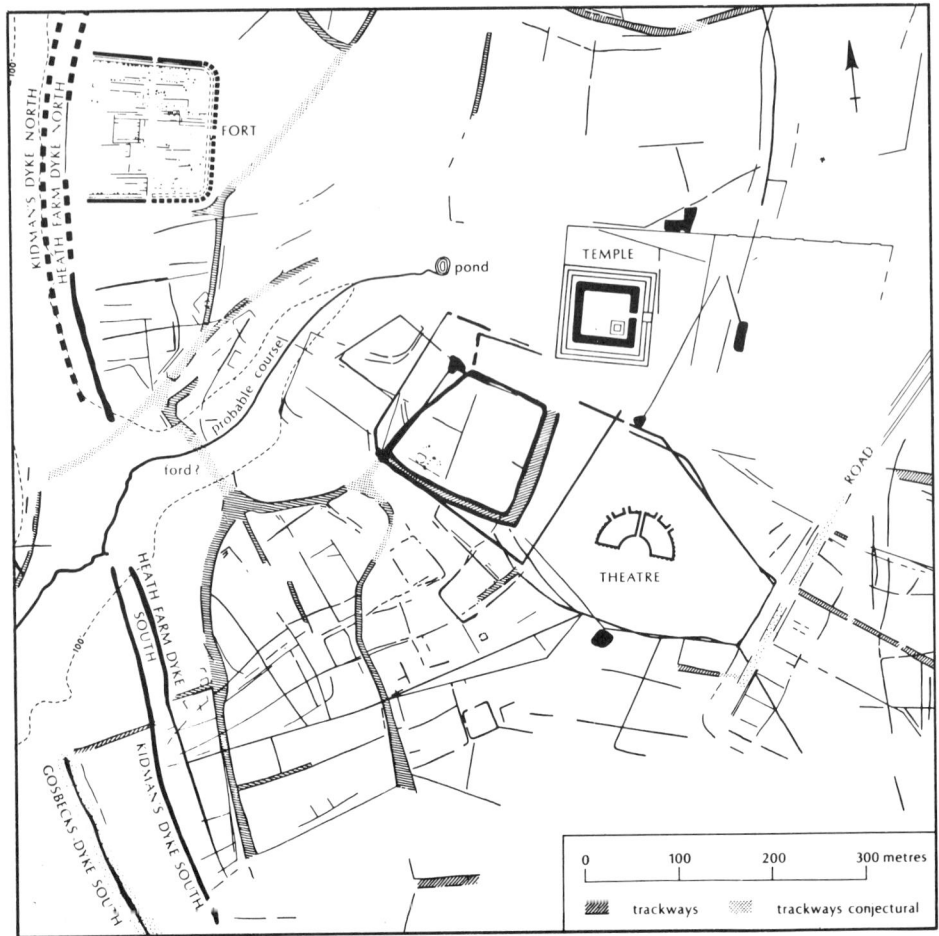

Plan of Gosbecks showing temple, theatre, trackways, fields, and dykes.

agricultural in character and many of the 'fields' may have contained a farmstead with its own houses, ancillary buildings, paddocks and enclosures, mirroring the occupation in the subrectangular enclosure itself.

To the north-east of the enclosure lay a sacred area, the focus of which may in the Celtic tradition have been a tree, a grove or a spring. In Roman times, the site continued to be regarded as holy and was dignified by the construction of the Romano-Celtic temple within a monumental 'double ambulatory' or corridor. To the south

was a theatre (p 19).

The single most exciting aerial discovery at Gosbecks was of a small Roman fort, first recognised in 1976 by Dr. D. R. Wilson of the Committee for Aerial Photography at the University of Cambridge, and independently by Mr. J. Hampton of the National Monuments Records, London. Although built against the innermost dyke at Gosbecks, the fort had been sited so that it caused minimal disturbance to the layout of the settlement. Its purpose was to control, not destroy.

THE ROMAN THEATRE WITHIN THE WALLS

An important feature of every large Roman town was its theatre, so the recent confirmation of the supposed site of the theatre at Colchester is a most significant step forward in the study of the Roman settlement.

The main body of the building was D-shaped in outline and about 70 metres in diameter. The curved part was the auditorium and the straight part the stage. Access to most of the seats was by a semicircular passage under the outer edge of the auditorium.

Although parts of the building have been uncovered on several occasions in the past, the discovery which led to its identification as a theatre was made in an area which in 1981 was being redeveloped for housing by the Colchester Borough Council as its 'Dutch Quarter Phase 3' scheme. Here, with the co-operation of the Borough Council and as part of a MSC Youth Opportunities Project, a small archaeological excavation was undertaken at a spot adjacent to where in 1891 several large foundations had been recorded, one of which was apparently curved. As a result of the excavation, parts of two foundations were revealed, five feet wide and curved to share a common centre. Between them was a well-preserved mortar floor which formed the base of a passage. When plotted and projected, the curved walls make a semicircle which fits perfectly between the presumed positions of the two north-south Roman streets known in this part of the town. The bar of the D-shape coincides in position and alignment

with the north wall of St Helen's Chapel which, as can still be seen today, incorporates a Roman wall in its base. Thus the plan, scale, and massive character of some of the walls leave no interpretation for the building other than a Roman theatre.

Maidenburgh Street, which crosses the eastern edge of the theatre site, was in a very poor state of repair so in 1984 the Borough Council replaced the road and pavements with a single surface of paved bricks. To do this, the existing surface and its make-up (all modern) had to be removed and as a result the foundations first seen in 1891 were again exposed. The foundations had been very cut about by modern services, especially for sewers. Nevertheless, more than enough survived to enable some valuable detail to be added to the plan of the theatre as then known. The foundations had lain so close to the modern street surface that in one place tar was still sticking to the Roman mortar. Also they had proved so tough and extensive that the

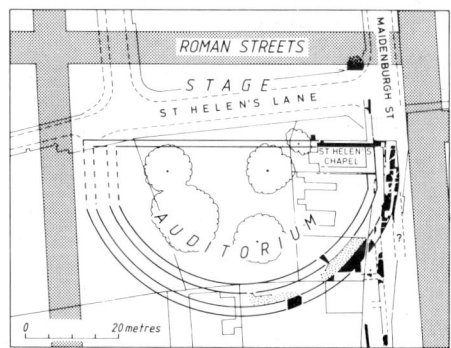

TEMPLE OF
CLAUDIUS
(remains
below castle)

TEMPLE PRECINCT

St. Helen's Chapel

position of Roman streets

walls
found here

THEATRE

private
houses

Excavations in progress in Maidenburgh Street in 1984.

builders of the Victorian cottages on the west side of the street did not attempt to remove them but built straight on top.

St Helen's Chapel has traditionally been associated with Roman times since in the so-called *Colchester Chronicle* (a brief, unreliable medieval text) we are told that the chapel was built by St Helena and restored by Eudo Dapifer, presumably in the late 11th or 12th century. The archaeological investigations in Maidenburgh Street not only confirmed that the north wall of the chapel incorporated a Roman foundation but showed that the base of the east wall of the chapel was also Roman. Thus the tradition in the Colchester Chronicle that the building was of Roman origin proves to have some basis in fact. Perhaps the chapel is more than simply a post-Roman building incorporating Roman foundations but a medieval conversion of upstanding remains of the theatre? But why in medieval times was part of the theatre thought to have been a Roman church? It is conceivable (although very unlikely) that the part of the theatre acquired some kind of association with Christianity in the later Roman period and that knowledge of this association survived until medieval times. Whatever the explanation, we can be sure that the link with St Helena is no more than medieval fantasy.

The theatre would have been able to house several thousand people probably seated on wooden benches and would have been used for the performance of Greek and Roman drama.

Across the street was the precinct of the magnificent Temple of Claudius so that together the group would have been an impressive sight. Tacitus tells us that Colchester had a theatre before the town's destruction by Boudica and her followers in AD 60/1. His theatre is likely to have been of wood and its remains may lie under those recently uncovered.

If anyone can be said to have to discovered the theatre at Colchester, it must be Rex Hull. On the basis of the 1891 plan, he firmly believed this to have been the site of the theatre but, despite some limited exploratory work in the 1950s, he was unable to obtain the necessary proof. Among his many achievements at Colchester, he was able to demonstrate by some deft trenching that there had been a timber theatre at Gosbecks, two miles from the town centre (pp 19 & 58). Since the sites of only four theatres are known in this country, Hull could be said to have discovered half the British examples!

Our work at Maidenburgh Street in effect continued where Rex Hull left off and such is the interest caused by the latest discoveries that the Borough Council has modified its building scheme to take them into account. The visitor to Maidenburgh Street can now see the well-preserved passage-floor and curved walls found in 1981 permanently on display in the ground-floor of one of the new houses and, with the aid of differently-coloured bricks, can follow the course of the outer wall in the new road surface.

IN SEARCH OF COLCHESTER'S PAST IN THE 1980s

The Culver Street site turned out to be the most rewarding excavation ever undertaken in Colchester town centre. Although similar in size to Lion Walk, the Culver Street site lies in a more critical position in relation to the Roman fortress and town, and the archaeological remains proved to be a great deal better preserved. The examination at Culver Street of Roman streets, the town defences, and parts of over twenty Roman buildings provided important new information on an unprecented scale about the history of the town.

The excavation started in 1981 on the sites of two Borough Council carparks, one to either side of Shewell Road. Difficulties and delays encountered by the developers during the run-up to the start of building works meant that the archaeological excavation had to stop in 1982 after the completion of the carpark sites and could not resume again for three years. The second and last phase lasted a brief but frantic year. The resources for the task were very inadequate so that the excavation effort had to be directed towards selected areas. Most of the work was concentrated on the site of the service basement, which, like its predecessor at Lion Walk, was to be two acres in size, about twenty feet deep, and thus necessitated the total destruction of all the archaeological remains on the site.

Before the excavation began, it was possible to predict the nature of the military and later remains likely to be encountered on the site. Although never identical, Roman fortresses of the mid 1st century and later run to a standard pattern so that once the limits, orientation, and some of the streets of a fortress are known, it is usually possible to guess some elements of its layout without any excavation. Occupying the central and thus the safest position of a typical fortress was the *principia,* the headquarters building. The principal transverse street passed along the front of this building and was called the *via principalis.* Making a T-shaped junction with the *via principalis* was another street, the *via praetoria,* which led from the centre of the front of the headquarters building to the principal gate.

Usually the barracks were grouped into units of six corresponding to a cohort of which there were ten to a legion. The six barracks comprising the accommodation of each cohort were generally arranged in a standard way: Blocks 1 and 2, 3 and 4, 5 and 6 faced one another across narrow streets with Blocks 2 and 3 and Blocks 4 and 5 being back-to-back. Each barrack block would have been 250 to 300 feet long and would have accommodated a company (or century) of about 80 men commanded by a centurion. The latter lived in comparatively spacious quarters at one end of his century's block. The barracks of the First Cohort (the most senior one) usually lay on the right-hand side of the headquarters building (when looking along the *via*

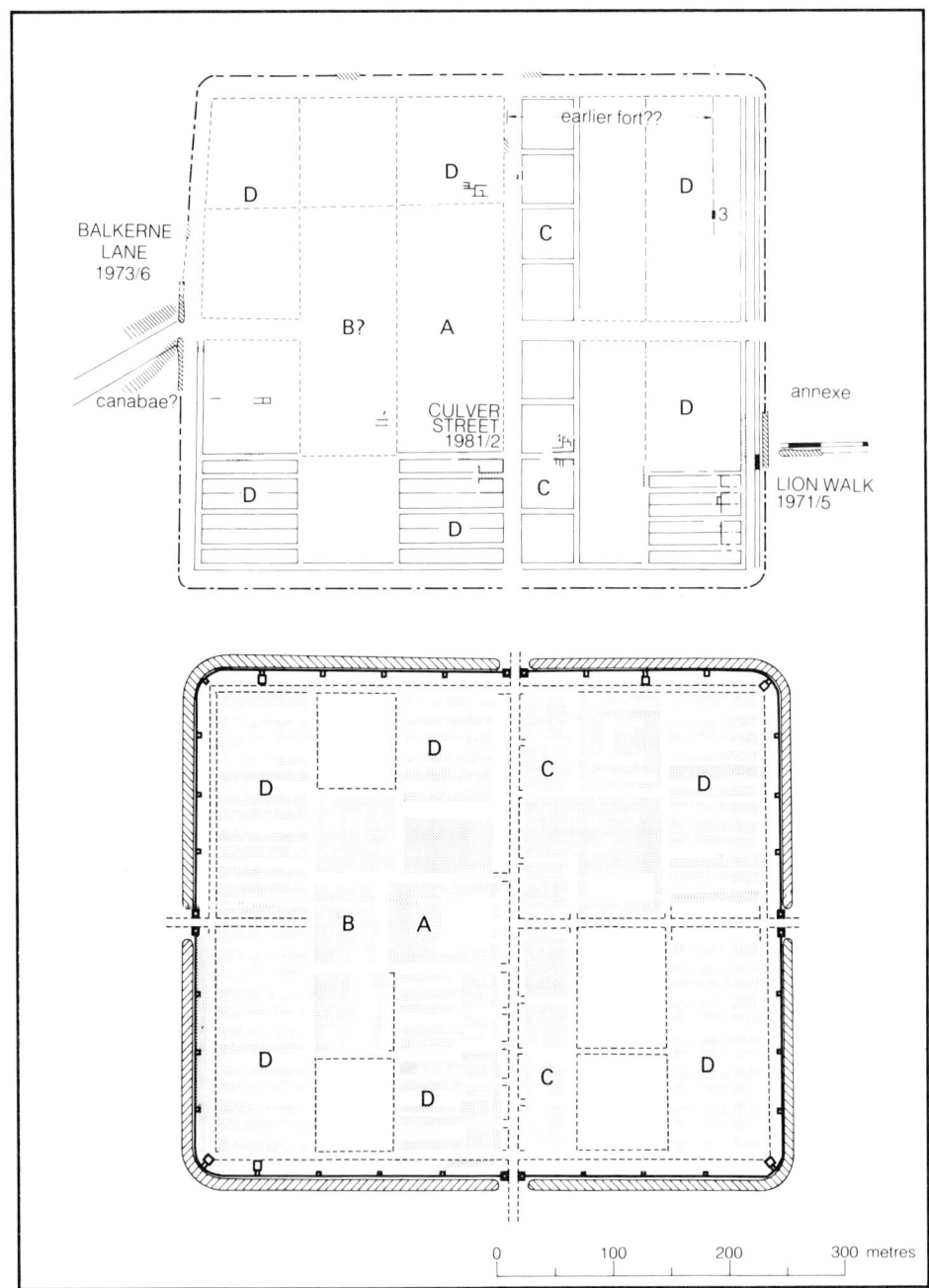

The fortresses at Colchester (*above*) and Caerleon (*below*). (Caerleon based on a plan by Mr G C Boon, published by permission of the National Museum of Wales.) A .... principia. B .... commander's accommodation. C .... tribunes' acccommodation. D .... barracks.

praetoria towards the gate) in such a way that the centurions' quarters lay alongside the *via principalis*. The commander occupied a large building either behind the *principia* or on the left-hand side of it whilst his six tribunes (junior officers above the rank of centurion), lived on the opposite side of the *via principalis* in six of the eight, roughly-square buildings which normally either lined the full length of its frontage or were separated from it by a row of storerooms. The reader will probably find the arrangement easier to understand by looking at the plan reproduced here of the well-explored fortress of Caerleon (which, as it happens, turns out to be surprisingly similar to Colchester in many respects.)

Prior to Culver Street, the work in Colchester had indicated that the fortress probably faced east and that the north-south Roman street which, at its southern end, passed along the centre of the Culver Street site and under the modern Shewell Road, originated as the *via principalis* of the fortress. This arrangement implies that the site of the *principia* must straddle the part of the present High Street 100 yards west of the town hall. Thus at the Culver Street site, on the west side of Shewell Road, there ought to lie the remains of the centurions' quarters of the First Cohort whilst the east side should be occupied by three of the eight large buildings which include the accommodation of the tribunes. And so it has proved to be.

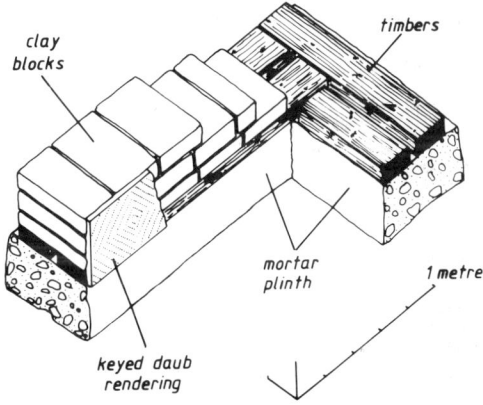

Stump of a military wall in a centurion's quarters at Culver Street.

In their expected positions were parts of all six barracks and two large buildings. The latter were probably tribunes' houses but, because only six out of the eight would have been used for this purpose, it is impossible to be certain about their function.

As at Lion Walk and elsewhere, the principal walls of the barracks incorporated low free-standing plinths. These were made by pouring a mixture of mortar and stones into wooden shuttering formed by two rows of planks set upright on edge in the natural sand. Timbers were placed along the plinth and above these were laid the unfired blocks of sandy clay which formed the body of the wall. The faces of the wall were rendered with a thin coating of daub which, on the inside face, was scored or impressed with

shallow grooves to provide a key for wall plaster. The purpose of the plinth was to provide a strong and stable base for the block wall and to raise it above the ground to prevent the foot of the wall being exposed to the damp. Because of the importance of the find, a large section of the plinth with its block wall has been boxed and lifted complete in that the hope that it will be possible to put it on display in the museum.

The internal walls were of a lighter construction and, like those at Lion Walk, seem mostly to have been of timber studwork with daub infill. Most of the floors were of sandy clay although in several of the rooms there had been wooden floors.

The parts of the barracks uncovered during the excavation had all been destroyed during the Boudican revolt thus indicating their reuse in the new town. Because they had been modified internally at various stages during their lifetimes, it is not always possible to be sure which modifications were military and which were civilian.

The ?tribunes' houses proved to have been very substantial buildings. They did not have any mortar plinths but instead had been constructed using a technique commonly met with on military sites in general but not until now found in a military context in Colchester. The

walls had been built by dropping large wooden posts into deep trenches. Thus although the life of the buildings would be limited because the bases of the posts would rot very quickly, the technique enabled the structure to be erected at considerable speed.

Parts of two ?tribunes' houses were uncovered as well as part of a narrow, east-west, gravelled street which separated them. The buildings probably measured about 130 feet square. Of the two examined, the southern building contained a range of rooms; several of these had hearths or small furnaces for brass-working suggesting that perhaps this building had been a workshop *(fabrica)* rather than a tribune's house. Neither of the buildings had been plastered and there were no indications of wooden floors.

Unlike the barracks opposite, these large buildings did not survive until the Boudican revolt. Both were demolished either by removing the posts or by sawing them off at ground level and leaving the buried stumps to rot. A new street (the same as the east-west one excavated at Lion Walk) was set out across the site of the northern building and new houses laid out on either side. The alignment of these new buildings was slightly different to that of the military fortress and matched the alignment of the eastern extension of the early town (p 81). They were timber-framed, had floors of sandy clay, and lacked any

Left: **Well-preserved remains of one of the walls of a centurion's quarters at Culver Street.**

mortar plinths.

With the Boudican fire came the complete destruction of all the buildings. The debris on the site of the northern barrack blocks was especially thick which is why several stumps of walls survived intact. After the fire, the streets were cleared of debris and, at the northern end of the site, new houses were erected on the original pre-fire plots. The narrow street, which originally had separated the northern barrack blocks, also survived the post-fire rebuilding operations to provide access along the rear of the new houses to either side of it. By contrast, the plots to the south were not built over but instead for the next century and more were used for cultivation. This discovery is very significant and, combined with the similar but less pronounced pattern of events at Lion Walk, shows that the post-Boudican town never managed to recover fully the vigour of its earliest days.

In time the new houses were replaced piecemeal as improvements were made or buildings were demolished because of decay. The latest houses were more substantially constructed and had mortar or rubble foundations and included tessellated and mortar floors. At least ten floors incorporated mosaics but none survived to any extent. One of the houses was very large. It measured about 120 feet across and consisted of four ranges of rooms around a central garden or courtyard. Underneath one of the rooms was a cellar with neat septaria and tile walls. The latter had been extensively robbed in the Norman period but in the rubble filling the remains of the cellar was a fragment of a marble table leg carved in the shape of a panther head. Scientific analysis has established that the source of the stone was the famous quarry at Paros in Greece. The piece would have been part of a very

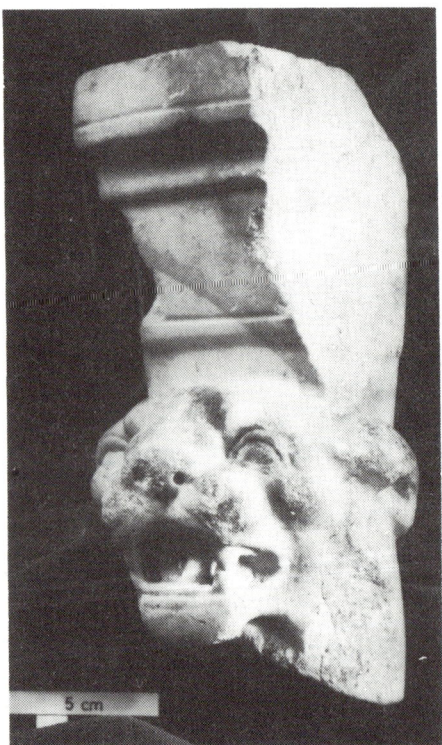

Part of the marble table leg carved in the shape of a panther head. From Culver Street.

68

Foundations and paved floors of Roman houses at Culver Street. The area covered by the photograph represents only about a fifteenth of the basement area and a thirtieth of the complete redevelopment site.

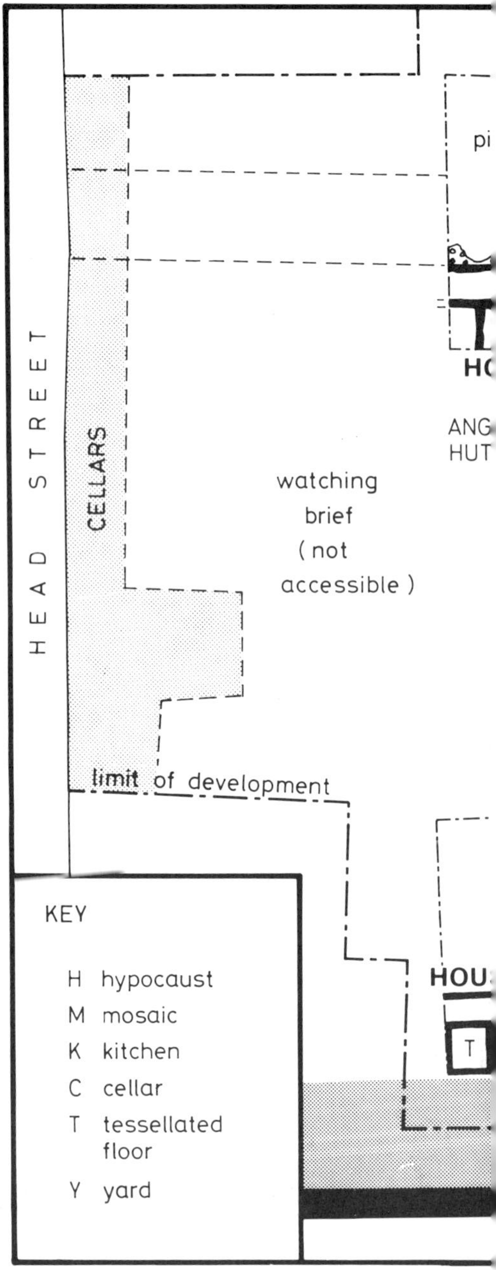

pi

HO

ANG
HUT

HEAD STREET

CELLARS

watching
brief
(not
accessible)

limit of development

HOU

KEY

H hypocaust
M mosaic
K kitchen
C cellar
T tessellated
   floor
Y yard

T

A mosaic being uncovered at Culver Street.

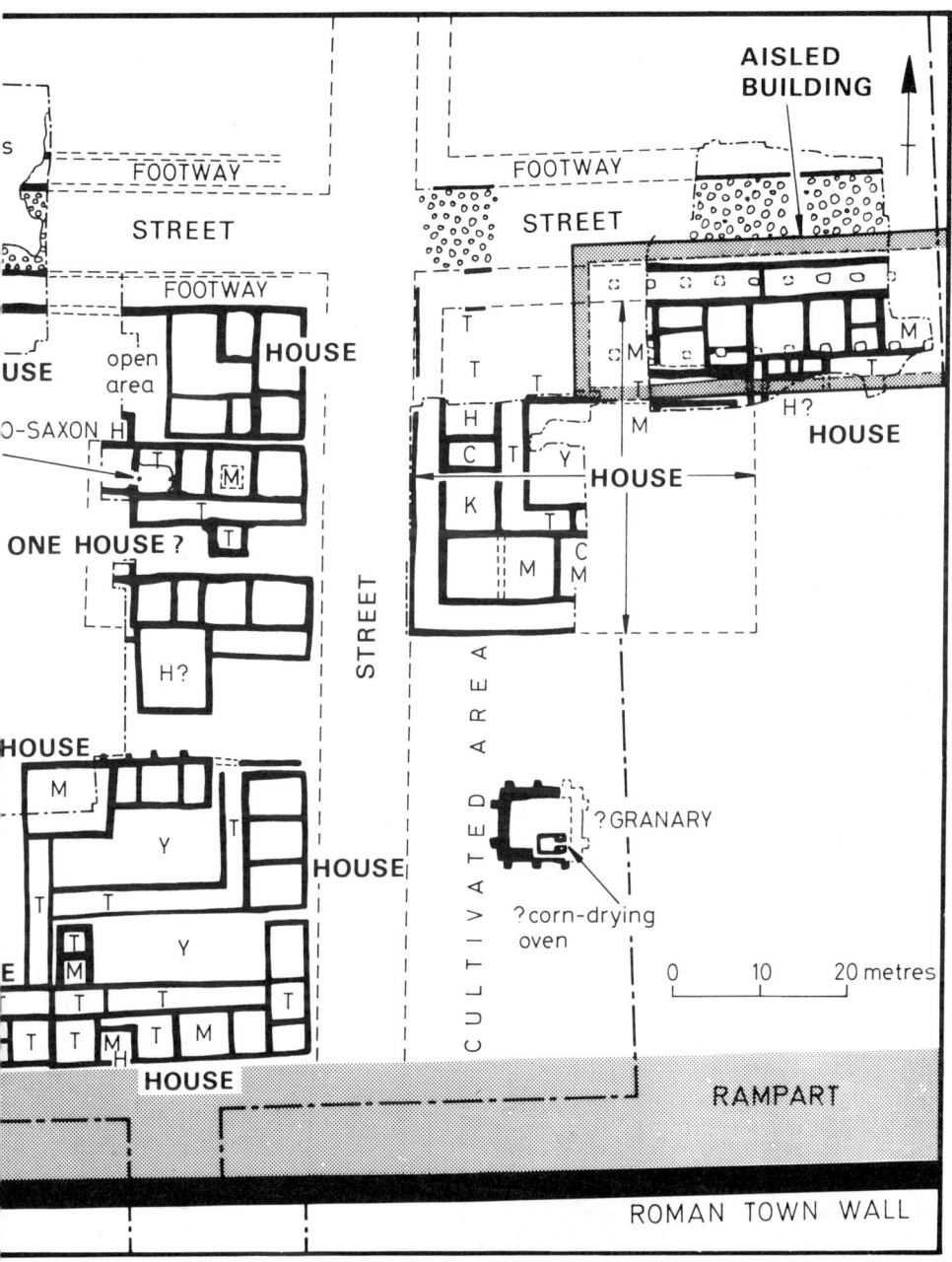

Provisional sketch plan of the latest Roman buildings excavated at Culver Street. The earliest of these probably dates from around AD 150.

expensive table made entirely of polished stone. The find is unique in Roman Britain and reinforces the conclusion evident from the size and quality of the building that it was the home of a wealthy family.

Probably in the 3rd century, houses were erected on the cultivated land on the west side of the north-south street. These turned out to be very well preserved and to contain an exceptional number of tessellated pavements. From this area came a few tiny fragments of a very delicate mosaic with cubes only about an eighth of an inch across. Again this was an unusual find because it is Colchester's first example of a mosaic intended for a wall rather than a floor. The cultivated area on the opposite side of the street continued in use throughout the Roman period and was never built over apart from a small granary and later a corn-drying oven made entirely of reused pieces of tile. Both structures are of kinds until now unknown in Colchester but are consistent with the agricultural use of the area.

A major and unexpected discovery was made on the area east of Shewell Road. At some time in the Roman period, probably in the 4th century, the private houses in this area had been demolished and their sites used for the construction of a large, aisled public building. The new structure was nearly 60 feet wide and at least 100 feet long with outer walls nearly five feet wide. The building covered the footway along the northern street frontage and encroached by several yards on to the street. Beneath the foundations of the walls and the aisles were dozens of wooden piles, up to six feet long, driven into the ground to provide the building with stability. Buildings of this type could have been used for a variety of purposes such as an exercise hall, a market or an administrative centre. But its plan, orientation (east-west), date, and the fact that its construction involved a change of use of the site suggests that it *may* have been a Roman church. The change of use is possibly the most significant of these features since, had the building been used for any other purpose, then the site would probably have been so used since the foundation of the town. Churches were first built in Britain in the 4th century at a time in Colchester when the construction of a large building may well have required the demolition of private houses to provide a large enough plot. Very few examples of Roman churches are known in Britain so that the enigmatic building at Culver Street is very tantalising.

Like Lion Walk, a length of the Roman town wall had to be removed to provide an access into the service basement under the shopping precinct. Before the wall was taken down, a trench on the site of the proposed entrance tunnel was excavated to examine and record the rampart and its underlying layers behind the wall. Not only did the excavation have to proceed side-

The aisled building at Culver Street showing the positions of the holes left by decayed wooden piles under the foundations of the aisles and outer walls.

ways rather than the conventional downwards, but working space was very limited because the roof of the new tunnel had to be in place before work could start. In the event, the excavation resembled a coal-mine; even a pneumatic drill had to be employed simply because there was not enough headroom to use the usual digging tools. Despite the difficulties, the work was very worthwhile. New dating evidence was recovered for the construction of the defences and further light was thrown on the building methods employed. And as a bonus, the face of the wall when finally exposed proved to be exceptionally well-preserved.

Following Lion Walk, Culver Street yielded an Anglo-Saxon hut. This is only the third one to be positively identified from Colchester. The hut dates to the 7th century or so and produced the largest group of Anglo-Saxon pottery found in the town so far.

Apart from early medieval trenches dug to remove stone and tile from Roman foundations, later activity was very limited. This is mainly because the site of the new service basement lies well back from the Head Street frontage where the nearest medieval and later buildings stood. (Shewell Road is 20th century in origin.) Consequently the Roman remains were comparatively undisturbed which is another reason why the Culver Street site proved to be so rewarding.

Whilst Culver Street was in progress, a smaller site at the Gilberd School was also being excavated. Its importance lay in the fact that the site provided the first opportunity in Colchester to excavate a large part of the men's quarters of a legionary barrack; hitherto the investigations at Lion Walk and Culver Street had been confined to the centurions' quarters of the barracks concerned. Originally there were fourteen compartments (known as *'contubernia'*) for the men. These lay east-to-west in a row and were separated from the adjacent street by a communal

The excavation of the tunnel behind the Roman town wall at Culver Street.

74

verandah covered by a roof supported on posts. Each *contubernium* measured about 22 by 11 feet and provided what must have been very cramped accommodation for eight men. In a typical legionary fortress, each *contubernium* was divided into two unequal parts. The smaller room is thought to have been used for the storage of kit whilst the larger one provided the necessary sleeping accommodation. But surprisingly most of the *contubernia* in the Gilberd School barrack had no internal subdivisions. Another curious feature of the building was that the timber drain, which lined the side of the street, appeared to lie along the inside of the verandah posts rather than between them and the street.

Although parts of the building seemed to have been standing at the time of the Boudican revolt, the barrack was not reused in the new colony like military buildings at Lion Walk and Culver Street. Instead a new street approximately on the same alignment as the eastern part of the town (p 27) was laid out 30 to 50 feet to the north and small buildings erected along the southern frontage of it so as to lie mainly between the barrack and the street. The longest building extended southwards by at least 80 feet. Because the land rises sharply to the south, the building was terraced into the slope with the effect that it cut through the centre of the barrack. Like the other buildings fronting the new street, the house was destroyed

A Roman gridiron from the Gilberd School site.

by fire in AD 60/1. A hearth in the burnt building incorporated a very fine gridiron of an unusual semicircular design which testifies to the skill of the Roman blacksmith who made it.

Apart from a few small buildings, the area seems largely to have remained as open land after the Boudican disaster. Being on the fringe of the town centre, the Gilberd School site provides yet further evidence like Lion Walk and Culver Street that the demand for building land after the revolt never matched that of pre-Boudican days.

THE DEVELOPMENT OF COLCHESTER

In towns such as Colchester, the archaeologist aims not only to unravel the sequence of the site on which he works but, more than that, he hopes to be able to translate his discoveries into terms of the town as a whole. In this way, he would hope to trace the development and character of the place with which he is concerned. For this reason the work of the 1970s and early 1980s at Colchester has been especially useful. From this and by studying previous excavations and other discoveries it is possible to postulate a sequence of development from the early days of Camulodunum to the present day. The result is in many respects conjectural — certain points will no doubt require revision and others may be proved to be wrong —but this does provide a framework for future work. Space does not permit the evidence for the sequence to be explained here but intrepid readers can find the information elsewhere (see the reading list at the end of the booklet). The likely stages in the development of the Iron Age settlement (*Camulodunum*) and the Roman town (*Colonia Victricensis*) are given in pictorial form on pages 74-5.

Interesting light has been shed on the way the military planner conceived the layout of the fortress. The discovery was made by taking various measurements of key distances on the most recent plan of the fortress (based on the Ordnance Survey 1:1250 plans) and converting these into Roman feet. From this it appears that first of all the planner set out on his plan a series of strips 300 and 200

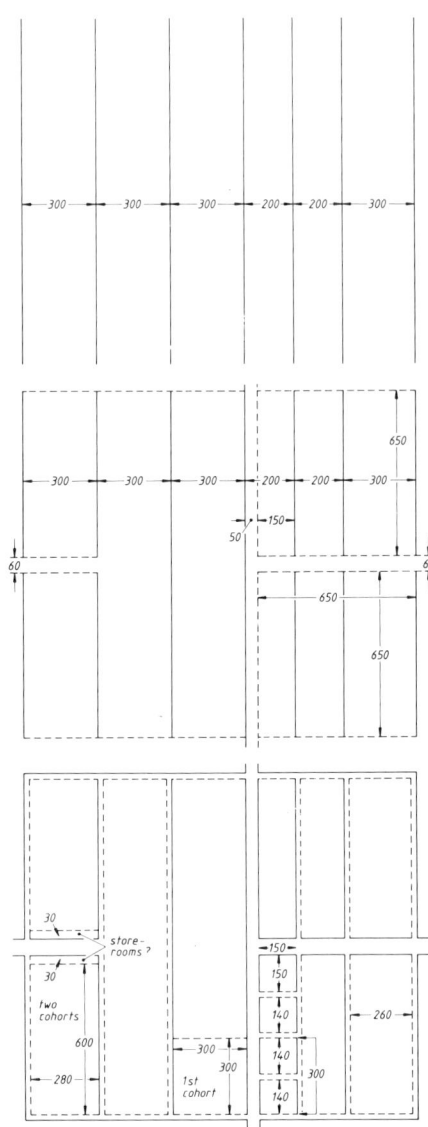

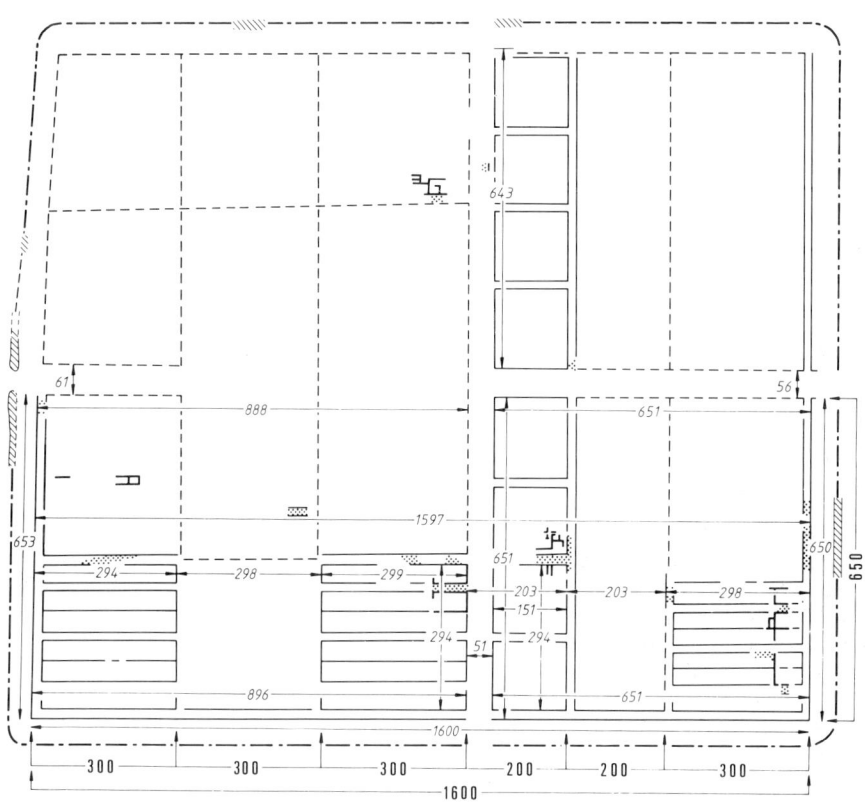

Above: **Measurements of the fortress at Colchester. The actual measurements are in italics. The intended measurements are shown in bold around the edge of the plan.**

Left: **Three stages in the formulation of the plan of the fortress at Colchester. Measurements in Roman feet (*pedes monetales*).**

Roman feet wide. Next he marked off the main streets. He then set out the northern and southern limits of the fortress and its main north-south minor streets by cutting these out of the 200 and 300 feet wide strips. Then he began to allocate plots for the individual buildings. Key distances measured on the modern Ordnance Survey plan prove to be very close to

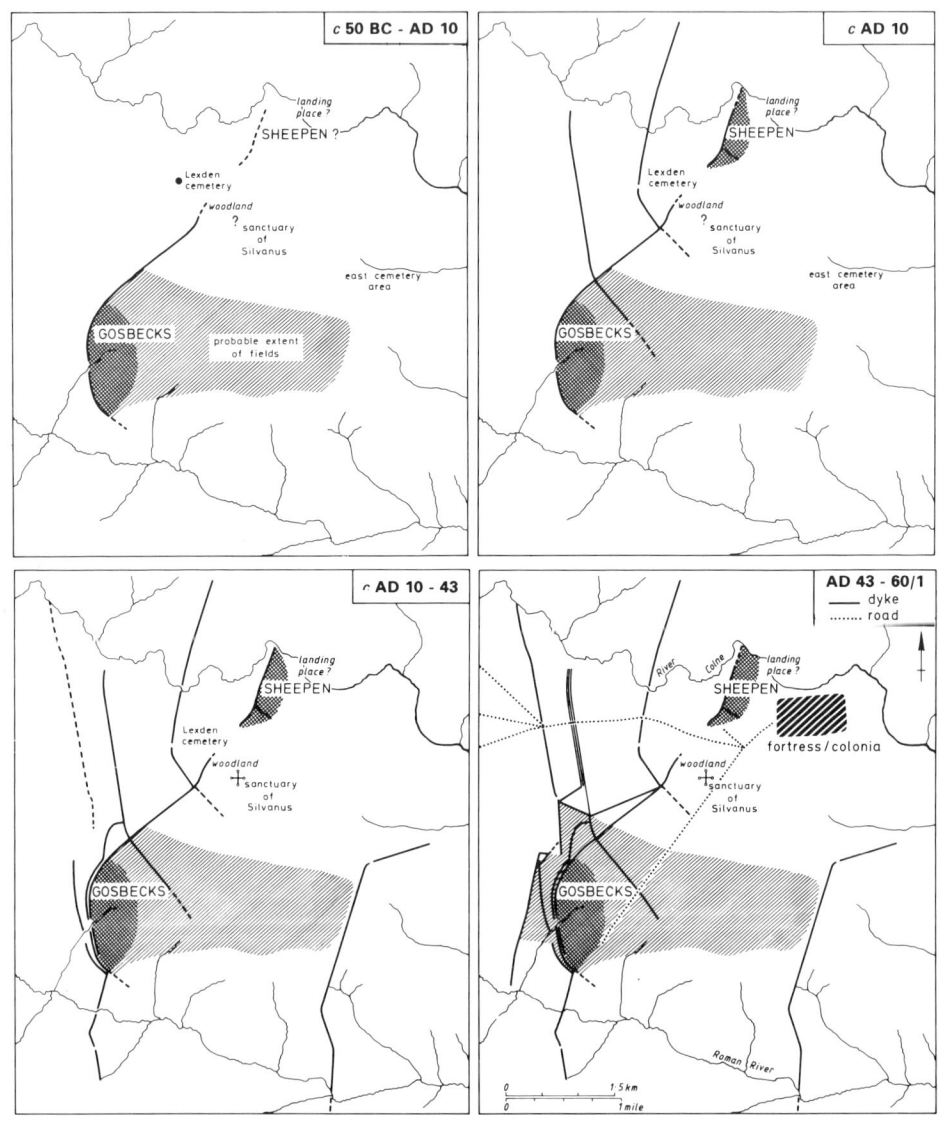

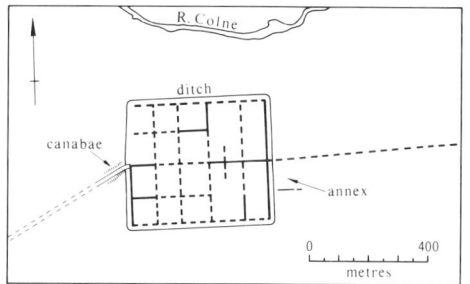

The fortress *c* AD 44-48.

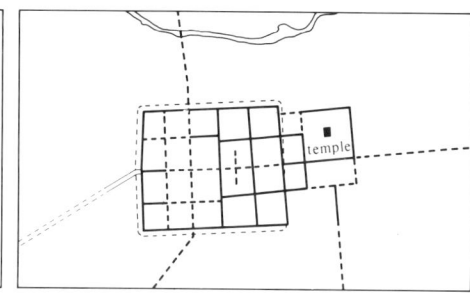

The colony *c* AD 49-60/1.

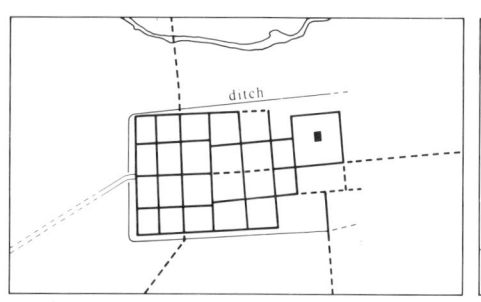

AD 60/1-*c* 80.

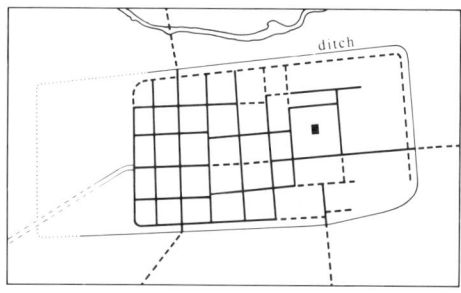

c AD 80-100/25.

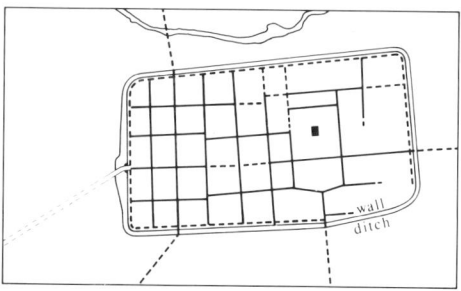

The early 2nd to the 5th century.

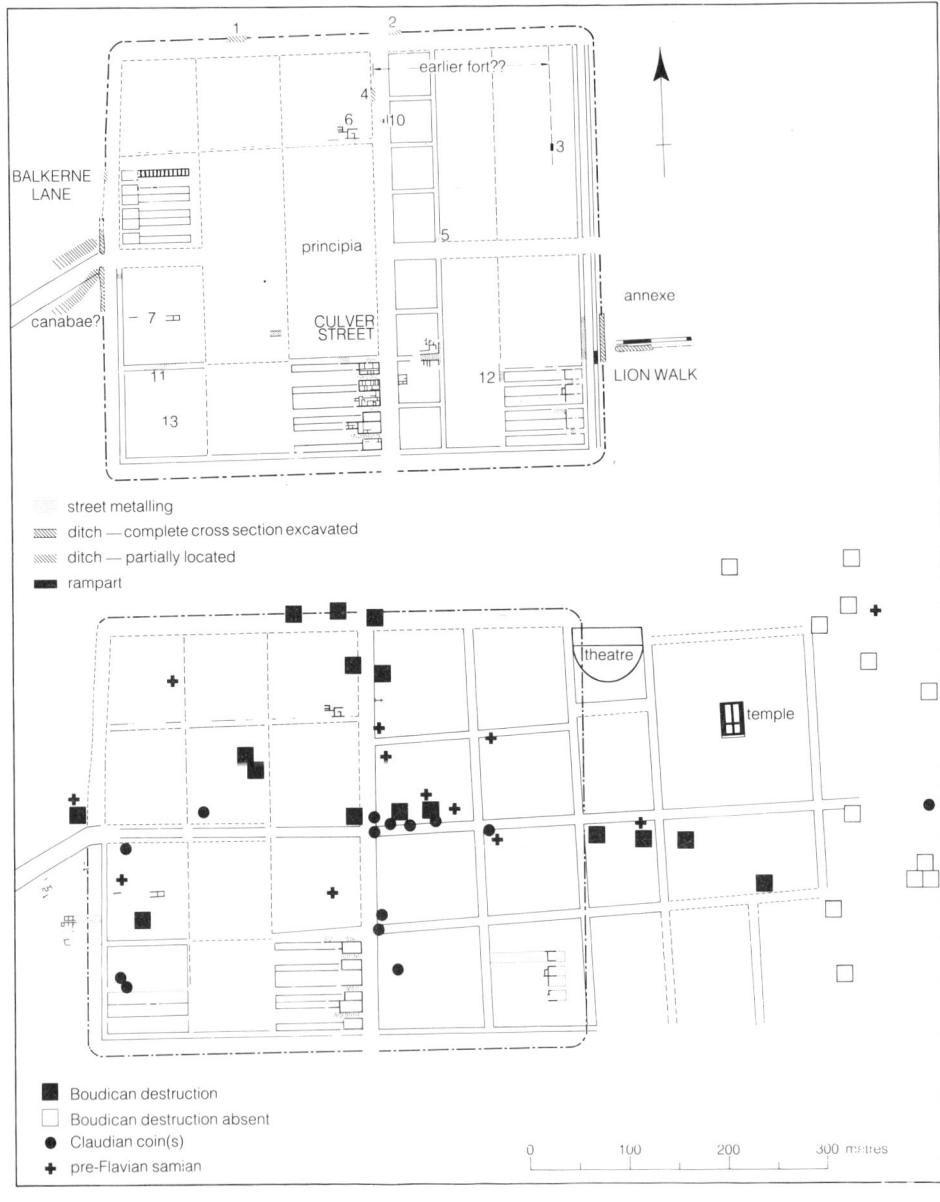

The conversion of the fortress at Colchester (*top*) into the town (*below*) before the Boudican revolt.

the theoretical distances based on the 200 and 300 feet wide strips so that the theory of how the fortress plan was conceived seems to be very convincing.

The manner in which the fortress was converted into a Roman town is of great interest and future excavations will no doubt reveal much more new information about this process. However it is quite clear that most of the military buildings were kept for reuse in the new town. Whilst this saved much effort in building new streets and houses, it meant that there was not enough room for the public buildings which the settlers wanted. To make the space, the surrounding bank and ditch which had protected the fortress was demolished and a new street grid was laid out on the eastern side of the town to incorporate the new public buildings. These included the Temple of Claudius, a town hall (probably immediately south of the temple), and a theatre (the probable site of which was confirmed at Maidenburgh Street in 1981). Unfortunately, the legionary defences were not replaced and the town was undefended at the time of the Boudican attack. The Roman historian Tacitus wrote, 'It seemed easy to destroy the settlement; for it had no walls. That was a matter which Roman commanders thinking of amenities rather than needs had neglected' (*Annals*, xiv, 32). Thus clearly excavation has confirmed Tacitus's statement about the absence of defences but what could the amenities be which he referred to? And what connection could there have been between these and the defences? The answer is that the amenities must have been the group of public buildings in the eastern part of the town and the 'neglect' was not so much the failure to construct new defences but the act of demolishing the existing ones so that the street grid could be enlarged and the 'amenities' constructed.

The disappearance of the Roman street grid after the end of the Roman period and the emergence of the present street pattern is a special problem not only here but in other modern towns on Roman sites. The layout of Colchester today is essentially as it was at least as far back as the 13th century; this is clear from the earliest written sources of the time where early forms of the street names appear. The most likely explanation for the loss of the Roman street pattern is that Colchester was completely replanned in the 9th or 10th century. This resulted in the loss of most of the vestiges of the Roman layout apart from the town wall and the position of the major gateways. This operation would have been instigated by the king in whose domain the place lay and may perhaps have been intended to stimulate the repopulation of what had become a decaying town. The Danes were in Colchester in the early 10th century but their role here is obscure. Possibly a Danish settlement was established in Colchester in the late 9th century and was destroyed in the early 10th by the English who then replanned the town.

In conclusion then, the study of Colchester has come a long way from distant days when antiquarians argued that Camulodunum was at Maldon. But much remains to be done. In the short term, there is still a backlog of finds from the excavations of the 1970s which needs to be thoroughly analysed, correlated, and published—a substantial task. From this will emerge much new information especially about the bone and pottery. In the long term, our conjectural sequence of town development needs to be improved and made more reliable, many Roman public buildings need to be found and excavated, particularly the public baths and basilica, and problems better understood such as the fate of Colchester at the end of the Roman period and the state of the town in the 8th and 9th centuries. Moreover no large area of Colchester has yet been completely excavated in detail. All the large-scale excavations of tho 1970s and early 1980s were incomplete since shortages of money and time prevented the thorough examinations that the sites merited. Only by excavating and recording in detail every redevelopment site threatened by destruction can a more complete picture emerge of the origins and development of Colchester. Our industrious predecessors have led the way and, provided we let no opportunities slip by, our accumulated knowledge can be further improved and enhanced towards a fuller understanding of Colchester's past.

ACKNOWLEDGMENTS

The pleasure of describing the work of others in Colchester is tempered only by having to omit so much. The limited space available has dictated that only a cursory summary of the course of archaeological research in the town has been possible and that the parts played by many individuals and societies has had to be barely touched on or left out entirely. For example, I am conscious of not having written of Sir W. Gurney Benham whose endeavours led to the publication of much of Colchester's earliest Borough records. Nor have I done justice to the Essex Archaeological Society for its important roles in the development of the Colchester and Essex Museum and the publication of much local archaeological material. Literally many hundreds, perhaps thousands, of people have contributed in some way or other ranging from M. R. Hull to those who have helped on an excavation or taken to the museum for recording an object found in Colchester. I hope this booklet will be regarded as a modest tribute to everyone, whether mentioned here or not, who over the years has helped bring our knowledge of Colchester to its present state.

The first edition of *In Search of Colchester's Past* was financed by appeal and a number of organisations responded in a generous way. These are the Colchester Borough Council, the Colchester Civic Society, the Friends of the Colchester Archaeological Trust, and Friends of the Colchester and Essex Museum, Friends' Provident Life Office, Frincon Securities Ltd (the two latter associated with the Lion Walk development), the Robert Kiln Trust, and the Royal London Mutual Insurance Society Ltd. The booklet is a longer version of a public talk sponsored and promoted by the Essex County Standard in November 1979. It was revised and enlarged in 1984.

For this booklet I am indebted to Bob Moyes who prepared many of the plans, to Alison Colchester for her photographic work, and to Peter Froste for his excellent and life-like drawings. Thanks are also owed to the staff of the Colchester and Essex Museum who have supplied some of the illustrations and provided facilities for others to be made. I am grateful also to Professor C. F. C. Hawkes for his help and guidance over the dykes and to Mr. D. T-D. Clarke for his assistance with various matters.

The excavations over the past thirteen years have been, because of their scale, a matter of teamwork. Adequate acknowledgment to all concerned can only made in the appropriate archaeological reports but to the following I owe special debts for their labours either on sites or indoors on post-excavation work: H. Brooks, E. Clark, A. Colchester, T. Cook, C. Crossan, G. Crossan, N. Crummy, S. Crummy, M. Daniels, A. Drysdale, L. Edwards, A. Gouldwell, J. Hind, I. Jenkins, R. Johnson, P. Kenrick, D. Lloyd, J. Lockett, D. Mann, R. Moyes, N. Oakey, D. Shimmin, M. Short, N. Smith, G. Summers, P. Sweeney, R. Symonds, S. Wade, K. Walker, and J. Whiffing. In addition, I am indebted to past and present members of CAT especially C. Buck, D. Clarke, M. Corbishley, Professor S. S. Frere, S. Maddison, I. McMaster, F. H. Thompson, Dr. M. Tite, and Professor J. J. Wilkes.

The success of an excavation, especially a large and protracted one, is dependent on the goodwill and assistance of the developer and contractor concerned. Regrettably the lengthy list cannot be set out here but our special thanks to the following must be noted: The Land and House Property Corporation Ltd and MacAlpines (Lion Walk); the Royal London Mutual Insurance Society Ltd, Fairclough Building Ltd and R.M. Douglas Construction Ltd (Cattle Market); Essex County Council (Butt Road); the Colchester Borough Council (Balkerne Lane, Culver Street, and the Roman theatre); Ipswich Roadworks (Balkerne Lane); the Carroll Group and Balfour Beattie (Culver Street). Similarly the success of the excavation programme itself is dependent on the help of various departments of the Borough Council and consequently our debt of gratitude is extensive here especially to the Departments of Engineering and Planning, the Treasurer's Department, the Town Clerk's Department, and of course the Museum.

Recent excavations have been financed by the Department of the Environment, the Colchester Borough Council and the Essex County Council with additional financial and other support from the Pilgrim Trust, Eastern Gas, the Lexden and Winstree District Council, the Land and House Property Corporation Ltd, the Royal London Mutual Insurance Society Ltd, the Colchester and East Essex Co-operative Society Ltd, the Carroll Group, Balfour Beattie, and many private individuals. Since 1976, projects funded by the Manpower Services Commission have played an invaluable role in rescue work in Colchester.

The Friends of the Colchester Archaeological Trust has provided valuable support for the work of the Trust. We are particularly indebted to the following for their help in this respect: C.Bellows, G.Chadwick, G.Corbishley, M. Corbishley, N. Crummy, and B. May.

SOME FURTHER READING — A SHORT SELECTION

Ideas and knowledge about Colchester's past are constantly being revised and improved so that publications are usually out of date even before the ink is dry. However, valuable accounts of various aspects of the town can be found in the following: *Roman Colchester* (1958), *The Potters' Kilns of Roman Colchester* (1963), both by M. R. Hull, *Camulodunum* (1947) by C. F. C. Hawkes and M. R. Hull, *The Trinovantes* (1975) by Miss B. R. K. Dunnett and *The Book of Colchester* (1978) by D. Stephenson. Although in many respects very out of date, a brief account of the 1971-4 excavations is contained in *Colchester, Recent excavations and Research* (1974) by P. Crummy. Detailed site reports are available in *Excavations at Lion Walk, Balkerne Lane, and Middleborough, Colchester, Essex* (Colchester Archaeological Report 3) by P. Crummy. *Aspects of Anglo-Saxon Colchester* (Colchester Archaeological Report 1) by P. Crummy is another technical publication in this case dealing with Colchester between about AD 450 and 1200. *The Roman Small Finds from Excavations in Colchester 1971-9* (Colchester Archaeological Report 2) by Nina Crummy catalogues many categories of Roman finds from the 1971-9 excavations. For up-to-date information about current excavations in the town, a twice-yearly newsletter can be obtained by joining the Friends of the Colchester Archaeological Trust (inquiries to Brenda May, 5 William Close, Wivenhoe, Colchester).

THE COLCHESTER EXCAVATION COMMITTEE

There have been four Colchester Excavation Committees. The first, founded in 1928 to continue the excavations in the Hollytrees Meadow, was followed by a second formed in 1930 to deal primarily with the Sheepen work although it continued for Hawkes's further excavations of the dykes area until the 1950s. The third committee was founded in 1950 to undertake two excavations, one in the Castle Park and the other behind the town wall, to mark the 1900th year after the foundation of Colchester. The fourth committee, now the Colchester Archaeological Trust, was formed in 1963 to cope with sites requiring rescue excavation mainly in the town centre.